I0803383

PAGE 1: THE BAMBOO CLUBHOUSE, CHENGDU, CHINA

ORO EDITIONS
Novato, California

HOW ARCHITECTURE TELLS

9 REALITIES THAT WILL CHANGE THE WAY YOU SEE

By Robert Tabin Steinberg FAIA

WITH **Gerald Sindell**

DESIGNED BY **Hoop Design**

INCLUDING MATERIAL BY **Susan Wolfe**

FOREWORD BY **The Hon. Penny Pritzker**

To Chocolate, Vanilla, and Strawberry and their mother, sweet, sweet Alice

MIRO TOWERS IN SILICON VALLEY. IN INTIMATE CONVERSATION WITH THEIR SMOOTH SURFACES FOR EACH OTHER, AND A DIFFERENT STORY FOR THE WORLD.
STEINBERG HART, 2021

FOREWORD THE HONORABLE PENNY PRITZKER

As a developer, I am well aware of the influence of architecture on experience. In 1979, my uncle Jay Pritzker and his wife, my aunt Cindy, established the Pritzker Prize, often dubbed the Nobel Prize for architecture. They believed that a meaningful architecture prize would encourage and stimulate greater public awareness of buildings and greater creativity among architects.

When Rob Steinberg phoned me to ask whether I would be willing to work with him as the developer of a new senior living community he was designing on the Stanford University campus, I was delighted to hear from my very dear childhood friend. Rob's father had designed the wonderful Atherton house I grew up in, and our families had become close.

At the time Rob called, I was primarily involved in hotels, but the timing was serendipitous as I had launched a business, called Classic Residences by Hyatt, which he believed offered the utmost elegance in senior living. This was the first company that I had started in my business career, and I felt from the start that design and architecture would be critical to our success, that making a place that felt both comfortable and functional, yet elegant and welcoming for our residents and their families was one of the keys to creating a successful community.

The Stanford project was intriguing to me because it was so very personal. I had grown up in Atherton and went to Stanford for law and business school. I cared deeply about the place where I had grown up and experienced so many good times. Rob brought to my attention this extraordinary opportunity to build the best-in-class senior living project on the Stanford campus, and thus we partnered together. Rob had enormous senior housing expertise and we brought the operational experience to the development.

Working with Rob, I saw a whole new side of the mischievous little boy I knew growing up. Rob was creative yet practical, focused, and extremely sensitive to the user experience — in this case, the senior residents, most of whom would sell their long-time homes in order to buy into this new senior community. For them, Rob wanted to recreate the gracious, California, indoor–outdoor lifestyle my parents, his parents, and our family friends had enjoyed in their single-family homes — in short, the type of home his own parents would find comfortable and enjoyable in an environment that would foster social interaction in their elder years. Coming from a hotel background, this was, of course, our company's sweet spot.

The resulting Classic Residences by Hyatt, now known as The Vi, has been featured in books and magazines the world over. It is the standard bearer for the highest quality in senior living. What a tremendous opportunity to help evolve the way our society cares for its seniors in later life. I was proud to be associated with the project, and with my lifelong friend, Rob Steinberg.

As a real-estate developer, I have worked with dozens of architects on a variety of projects. Rob's skill at sculpting spaces that bring people joy is truly a gift as he leaves a little piece of his heart in every project. On a broader scale, Rob's talent in using spaces to help shape lives has led to an enormous body of architectural work that spans the state of California, the United States, and the nation of China. Rob learned from his father how much space matters to people's lives, and how creating comfortable and enjoyable environments fosters social interaction and greater connection. Rob and I also share the experience of being the second generation to work in our family businesses. We know that values and integrity are critical to success and vital for a sustainable enterprise, especially one that is family-led.

We also know the high expectations that come with working with the ones we love the most. It was incredibly fun to be the second generation of our families working together.

Rob is a storyteller and a dreamer. In the pages that follow, you will read of his dream to transform his father's well-respected, small architecture firm into an international titan, taking the primary practice from custom, wood-frame homes to concrete, steel-and-glass high rises.

In the process, he was also transformed — from a mischievous boy into a renowned thought leader in the field of architecture.

THE HONORABLE PENNY PRITZKER
U.S. Secretary of Commerce, 2013–17
Founder and Chairman, PSP Partners

THE SUBLIME
HAZING

The Home and 'The House'

At the same time that he opened his architectural practice in 1953, my father, 'Goody,' speculated with virtually all of his money designing a grand home on six acres of hilltop land in Los Altos Hills. But as construction neared completion, Goody was running short of funds necessary to pave the half-mile-long, winding road to the crest of the hill where the house was situated. The *For Sale* sign went up, but when prospective buyers spun out and gave up on the terrifying gravel road, Goody decided our family could no longer afford both the mortgage payments on the grand-spec house as well as the rent on our home near town. Goody closed the lease and moved our family up the hill, where I was raised in splendor.

It turned out to be the best thing Goody could have done for his career. Suddenly everyone viewed him as a success, living in a dream home, though admittedly at that time, in a neighborhood that was regarded as "way out in the country." In contrast to the bland, low-slung ranch homes proliferating across the region's flatlands, Goody's modern sensibility melded the organic and natural world of Frank Lloyd Wright with the refinement and exquisite proportions of Ludwig Mies van der Rohe.

The house incorporated enormous plate-glass windows, some stretching 18 feet high, which offered sweeping views of the picturesque valley below. Stone floors spanned from indoors to out, a massive fireplace wall anchored the living room, and rich wood-soffitted ceilings offered a refined elegance. Bedrooms opened to private patios and an elevated swimming pool that was cantilevered off the hillside. A stable adjacent to the home housed our horses; ducks and geese animated the gardens, and an orchard on one side of the property provided an abundance of apricots. A meadow at the foot of the acreage, in the right season, was populated by a profusion of colorful butterflies.

Santa Clara County was at that time called, without irony, "The Valley of Heart's Delight." Our lifestyle meshed beautifully with the new world emerging there — the very clientele that Goody hoped to attract to his practice. Annually my parents hosted back-to-back Friday and Saturday night grand dinner parties, getting double-duty use from the rented tables and chairs, the flower arrangements, linens, and other accoutrements needed to entertain a large crowd. Catered by the best chefs, the food was consistently fabulous. Some of the guests were friends or colleagues who had entertained my parents; some were stakeholders in large, upcoming projects; some were well-to-do prospective individual clients for custom homes; and some were those corporate clients, like Ampex, Hewlett Packard, and Intel that would eventually give the area a new name: Silicon Valley. All came away with the sense that if Goody was so accomplished that he could build such a home and standard of living for himself, why not for them, too?

Orders for work began to come in, and Goody's practice was soon thriving.

My life, in many ways, was magical. My surroundings made me acutely aware of the land and how the 'built environment,' or man-made, intertwined. My mother, Gerry, loved nature, and each year on her birthday we took a family hike and enjoyed a picnic behind our house on one of her favorite trails in the Rancho San Antonio Open Space Preserve.

After school I often rode my horse, Duke, down from our home in the hills to the Rancho Shopping Center in the Los Altos flatlands abutting the train tracks — this was well before Foothill Expressway was built. There, my friends and I would enjoy sodas and French fries. All of the middle school girls my age loved horses, and I loved all of the girls!

With an architect father, the arts were threaded through everything. I played piano and clarinet, and had weekly art lessons from a Stanford professor.

OPPOSITE THE AUTHOR, LEFT, WITH HIS SISTER'S HORSE, REBEL, RIGHT.

RIGHT FROM LEFT, THE AUTHOR'S SISTER JOANIE, MOTHER GERRY, FATHER GOODY, BROTHER TOM AND THE AUTHOR, AT THEIR FIREPLACE, C.1958.

By junior high school I was making short art films and movies of our family vacations. By high school I was a passionate photographer and began acting.

The Pritzkers

Coming from Chicago, my parents were well acquainted with the wealthy and often brilliant Pritzker family. One of the three sons, Don, was the baby of the family and the "rebellious" son. After graduating from Harvard with a bachelor's degree and earning a law degree from the University of Chicago, Don and his wife, Sue, moved to California, where the family put him in charge of their recently acquired Hyatt hotel chain.

Don and Goody ran in the same social circles and soon became business colleagues, as Don hired Goody to design a grand, 12,000-square-foot Atherton home and some of the early Hyatt hotels, including the Del Monte Hyatt in Monterey.

As Goody worked with Don and Sue, the couples became close socially. Goody's design for their residence became his master treatise on contemporary California architecture, including his signature stone, wood, and glass vocabulary and Wright-inspired detailing. The home was designed for entertaining, and the Pritzkers put it to full use.

I got to know the compound well, as the Steinberg family soon found ourselves at the top of the invitation list to the Pritzkers' frequent weekend gatherings. The Pritzkers owned a theater-in-the-round in Burlingame, across the street from Don's office, and the performers often ended up in the social mix at their house. Walter Mondale was a regular before he became Vice President. We were sometimes treated to a spontaneous performance by actors, comedians, and musicians, including jazz great Louis Armstrong.

The Kennedy-esque summer fun included touch football, barbecues, tennis, and swimming, all capped off with hot fudge sundaes from the 1950s-style soda fountain. Although you could often find Sue and Don Pritzker in black tie apparel on a weeknight, entertaining dignitaries of one stripe or another, come the weekend, they were out on the lawn playing touch football along with my parents and all six of us kids. Penny Pritzker is like a sister to me to this day.

Rebellion

The bad news about having a horse was that Goody assigned me the job of cleaning the manure out of the stable on Saturday mornings. My brother and sister had chores, too, but mine struck me as punitive. Tom watered the plants. Joanie emptied the dishwasher. I shoveled shit.

Part of me loved and respected my father. He was inquisitive and spontaneous; he lived in the moment and enjoyed life to the full. He had a philosophy and set of principles that gave structure to how he attacked and solved problems. He played sports with us kids, and encouraged — I dare say, demanded — that we do our best. There was something quite endearing about him, too. He never held back. He was deeply involved in our lives, and very supportive.

Integrity meant everything to Goody. If he gave his word, he kept it, no matter what, and he expected nothing less from others. He cared a great deal about his community. I admired these qualities and wanted to emulate them.

The part of me that had a harder time with my father was my strongly rebellious temperament: I took after my father in this regard, wanting to do what I wanted to do and stubbornly resisting what I did not. He was very tough, and I bristled in kind and became tough, too.

GOODY STEINBERG, ARCHITECT.

GERRY STEINBERG, FIRST FEMALE SANTA CLARA COUNTY SUPERVISOR.

He demanded perfection. When my siblings and I brought home our report cards, Goody zeroed in on the one "B" rather than praise the five "As." Excellence was expected; weakness was to be remedied. As a result, I grew up walking on eggshells, ever fearful of getting in trouble.

Goody was opinionated and headstrong, which made me want to argue with everything he said. He was always certain that he was right, which meant that any dissenting opinion, especially coming from me, was wrong. We were often at loggerheads, with arguments erupting at the dinner table, in the car, or wherever he wanted to lecture me on something — school, the Vietnam War, or what it meant to be a success. I pushed back, and neither of us cared who else was in earshot.

Until somewhere around 6:30PM every evening, I lived in paradise. But when Goody came home, the atmosphere shifted. Dinner at 11280 Magdalena Road came to be known as "the inquisition." My sister, my brother, my mother, and I — and often a friend or two — took our places around the table only to submit to the full force and focus of Goodwin. Each diner was called upon in turn to present and explain the events of the day while Goody sat in cool judgment, sharply questioning, determining whether the presentation was up to snuff or lacking.

"What did you do today?"

"Was it acceptably productive?"

"Could you have handled anything better?"

"What did you learn?"

The sense of relief when his attention turned to the next victim was mitigated only by compassion for the unfortunate next to risk his interrogation. "The inquisition" gave everyone present a stomach ache, but one thing I learned from this nightly ordeal was: be prepared! I knew what questions were coming my way. I knew what was expected when my turn came to face "the inquisitor." As my early teen years progressed, I questioned myself throughout the day whether my pursuits had been productive enough and how I might have better managed the ups and downs that came my way.

The tyranny even extended to our wonderful live-in housekeeper, cook, driver, and nanny, Martha. If the dinner plates were delivered to the table in a way that was not aesthetically balanced, my father would send them back to the kitchen. Besides being delicious and nutritious, the items on the plate had to be positioned and proportioned in a visually appealing way.

My sister Joanie was not permitted to leave the table until she'd eaten every pea on her plate. She would wait until Goody's focus was elsewhere — often scolding or arguing with me — and quietly slip the peas, one by one, into her napkin until her plate was clear.

Mom

I often wondered why my mother went along with the obstinate way that Goody ruled our roost. Gerry was a strong, independent, highly educated woman. Yet at home she was careful, cautious, rarely interceding on her children's behalf. Perhaps because she was from a generation in which women hesitated to contradict their husbands, she was reticent to step in to save any of us from his wrath.

My mother went to Stanford Law when I was a child — one of only four women in her class. She then went into public life, and became a leader in the Santa Clara County government. So in those days I really didn't know her well. Much of what I knew about her came from the local newspapers, where I was proud to

THE AUTHOR, JUNIOR VARSITY SOCCER, MOUNT HERMON SCHOOL FOR BOYS.

read about her accomplishments in saving the great unspoiled green areas that take up much of the land around Silicon Valley, a gift to the region that will continue to enrich generations.

Although we would not create a strong bond until much later in life, her gifts to me at that time were essential. Being a persuasive public speaker herself, she taught me how to stand and how to gesture in order to hold an audience, whether I was reciting Kipling's "If" or giving a report on how I spent my summer. My mom's father had been a highly regarded women's clothing manufacturer, and from that world she instilled in me an understanding that in order to gain respect I always had to look the part. She dressed me with great care, and my passion for rebellion did not include self-neglect.

Banishment

Without her intervention, my run-ins with Goody became frequent and so explosive that my mother said she worried we might actually come to blows. With my father and I finding it increasingly difficult to live with one another, a friend of Goody's touted an East Coast boarding school his children attended and where he served as a trustee. It seemed like a way out for all of us, and we agreed I should attend the prep school. Goody felt that an East Coast academy would provide an excellent education, surround me with the "right type of people," and prepare me for a productive life. I believed that getting out from under Goody's surveillance and house rules could only offer an improvement over life as I knew it in the near (but not near-enough) paradise of my parents' home.

At the tender age of 14, my parents put me on an overnight flight to Boston's Logan Airport. I then took a three-hour bus ride out to Mount Hermon, Massachusetts, where I knew not a single soul.

The Mount Hermon School for Boys was like going to a foreign country. The others spoke a language and lived a culture completely alien to me. I struggled with the rigors of the academic program. Socially, too, I felt isolated. Although I lived in a cottage of 25 students, I was left without a built-in buddy when my roommate called it quits after I had been there just six weeks. Eventually I made a couple of close friends, and the isolation eased.

With my California aesthetic — blue sneakers, casual shorts, and a general oblivion to symbols of status like clothing labels, high-end cars, and the names of swanky Connecticut suburbs — I developed a somewhat exotic California/preppy hybrid identity distinctive enough to win election as class president. But the constrained school environment left me unhappy.

Mount Hermon relied on the teachings of its evangelical founder, the Reverend D. L. Moody. The Bible was a primary classroom tool, accompanied by a challenging academic program on a par with other elite private boarding schools. Manual labor was required of all students, whether janitorial, laundry, kitchen, or farm duty. Mandatory chapel attendance four times a week, a coat-and-tie dress code, and strict compliance with reveille and lights-out were the orders of the day. I quickly discovered that I did not take well to following a rigid regimen. I needed my freedom to be who I was, to express myself, and to do what I wanted without boundaries and restrictions. I was beginning to understand that I would never thrive within an authoritarian environment.

I groused about Mount Hermon's closed campus — we were permitted to leave the grounds only once per quarter. But the truth was that there was nowhere to go: the school was isolated 100 miles east of Boston on the Vermont border. I built no bond with a single faculty member. I saw no one who could function as a role model.

I felt as if I was in purgatory.

When I came home for winter and summer breaks, I was tormented by all that I was missing: the freedom and experimentation of the Bay Area in the 1960s. And then I would return to what I saw as "reform school," always aching to bust out. A close friend had been similarly banished to Deerfield Academy, 20 minutes from Mount Hermon, and we commiserated together. We both were unhappy with our respective prep schools but kept our thoughts to ourselves when his parents came out to visit and took me out to dinner, or when mine came out and took him with us to eat.

During my summers at home, when I wasn't working at Goody's architecture firm for pocket money — gardening, filing blueprints, running errands — I joined my old friends in their much less restrained, anti-establishment pursuits driven by raging hormones, consisting of lots of pot, abundant alcohol, sexual experimentation, and the music scene. My best friend turned 16 nearly a year before I did, which meant he got his driver's license, and we were free at last. San Francisco beckoned, and the inviting aromas of Haight Ashbury and the illuminating sounds of The Fillmore — Big Brother & the Holding Company, Janis Joplin, Jefferson Airplane, Santana, and Grateful Dead — were suddenly within reach.

I stuck it out at Mount Hermon for as long as I could, but came home after two-and-a-half years, at the semester break of my junior year of high school. At first I felt as if I had a great failure on my shoulders, something I might never outlive. But gradually I came to see that it was just a really bad fit. Too much was dictated. There was just so little leeway to express myself.

A Business Mentor

Back at home in Los Altos Hills, I enrolled at Awalt High School in Mountain View, where I took advantage of a work-study program that allowed me to schedule my classes in the morning and spend my afternoons working off-campus. Initially, I stocked the shelves at Sammy Kahn's pharmacy in downtown Los Altos, and delivered prescriptions and sundries to local nursing homes and senior care facilities.

Later, I went to work after school for a family friend, Stuart Moldaw, a gifted entrepreneur and early venture capitalist. I stocked merchandise and delivered inventory to his Country Casuals and The Colony clothing stores (the forerunner to Ross Department Stores). I admired Stuart's approach, which diverged dramatically from my father's. Stuart was a button-down New Englander, precise and meticulous. I was an artsy hippie, yet he took me under his wing. I tagged along as he walked through the warehouse in suit and tie, ensuring things were running smoothly and making himself accessible to employees at every level. It was not uncommon for him to stop and inquire, "How are things going for you?" or "Are you learning anything?" of an inventory or delivery clerk. Stuart was a successful businessman. My father saw himself as an artist. I wanted to be both.

Still at War

Two-and-a-half years at boarding school had done nothing to abate the tensions between me and Goody. With the threat of being drafted and dying in Vietnam, my friends and I felt we were fighting for our lives. We held our breath that day in 1969 as the draft numbers were announced. Each number was a live bullet for someone in a game of Russian roulette.

It seemed that everything I did aggravated Goody. I bought a fabulous hot-rodded Chevy that just needed a little work, and he declared it to be a money pit. Like my father, I smoked cigarettes, but no matter how much I tried to hide it, he always seemed to find me and ground me for ever-lengthening stretches. I thought that the U.S. was murdering women and children in Vietnam; he thought it was a necessary war that justified almost anything. I did not hesitate to denigrate his view of success (which was basically what he had achieved), and he thought I was rebelling for the sake of rebelling.

When I couldn't take it, I would depart home abruptly, without leaving word of my whereabouts. I was rudderless, staying with friends until tensions subsided or my mother intervened. I ran away a lot — often to the home of my math tutor, but once to Los Angeles. Only through the persuasive powers of my mother, who flew down to retrieve me, did I finally agree to return home.

False Start

Goody decided on the college I was to attend in the same way that he selected Mount Hermon School for Boys: he had a friend who sat on the board of trustees of Grinnell College, Iowa, who enthusiastically recommended it to him. But being a theater major at a liberal arts college in the middle of nowhere was for me about as good a fit as Mount Hermon. Despite my fast AMC Javelin, my membership on the golf team, and a serious girlfriend, I struggled to find my place and genuine interests. I was not as rigidly boxed in as I had been at Mount Hermon, but the isolation was brutal. I became convinced that I was not cut out for the agricultural heartland or for higher education.

A First Career

And then, in May 1970, as protests against the bombings in Cambodia gave rise to protests on campuses across the country, four Kent State students were shot by the Ohio National Guard. Grinnell shut down and I was delighted to tell my parents that they should save their money: college was not for me.

Goody would have none of it, and, together with Stuart Moldaw, helped push me in the direction that would lead to my first career.

"You must go to college," Goody insisted. Although he wanted to pressure me to become the third-generation Steinberg architect, he took the risk of trying to discover what actually might be *my* preference. "What do you love to do?"

"I love going to the movies," I answered.

He suggested film school, typically insisting that I must choose between the top two in the country: the University of Southern California or the Tisch Program at New York University . I was accepted by both, and Stuart, my trusted mentor, had strong feelings about NYU.

"An East Coast experience in a sophisticated, urban city will give you a perspective different than any you've had so far. New York will broaden you."

Stuart was right. I went to NYU, and both the school and the city had a profound impact that altered my life. The first lesson came just hours after arriving. My brand new, very expensive, Bolex film camera was stolen as I made my way from the airport to my temporary digs while waiting for the dorms to open.

The theft of my camera delivered a blunt introduction to the grittiness of New York life. But soon enough, the richness of the NYU program kicked in and my enthusiasm for life in the hotbed of non-conforming, free-thinking creativity and urban sophistication took over.

I started mid-year at NYU, as was becoming the story of my life, and cliques were already set. But every morning I would get up, get dressed, and go to class, where … we watched movies! Later, the class would discuss each film: the lighting, the camera angles, the sound, the direction. And, most importantly, we talked story. How the writer and the director crafted the audience experience, from the opening shots that set the tone, to the whole notion

FROM LEFT, THE AUTHOR, A FAMILY FRIEND, JOANIE, GOODY, TOM AND GERRY IN THE RANCHO SAN ANTONIO OPEN SPACE PRESERVE.

of themes and development, and the use of tableaux to set a transition to the next major part of the story.

At night, we worked on our own films. In those pre-computing days, strips of film festooned the walls of the editing suite, and late into the night I would be splicing by hand, reviewing shots or scenes and occasionally scrambling around to find a shot that had temporarily been lost to the cutting-room floor.

Alice

I lived in a dorm called The Brittany on West 10th Street. Walking down 4th Street, where Bob Dylan and Andy Warhol were breaking all the rules in the arts scene, was mind-expanding. The education outside the classroom was every bit as eye-opening as the learning gleaned in film school. Soon enough I began to make friends. Michael Carlin was a long-haired, mustachioed Italian who hailed from Atlanta. He introduced me to a Jersey girl, Alice Erber, who was also in the film school pursuing a focus in editing and sound. Michael said she needed a cameraman on one of her projects and thought I might be willing to help.

We first met at a basement macrobiotic bakery, and, from the start, she hit all the right receptors for me. We became great friends long before our relationship took a romantic turn, exploring Greenwich Village, enjoying pasta dinners, discovering the sights in Chinatown, exploring art galleries and dissecting films, from the avant-garde to the classics. Alice lived on Horatio Street, a block from the West Side Highway, which at that time was home to junkies and prostitutes. I was actually afraid to go over to her place. As a precaution, she carried a dollar in her shoe to appease any mugger who might threaten her. We soon became inseparable.

Before long, Alice and I, Michael and his roommate Eric Magnuson began creating films as a foursome.

When I wasn't working on films, I worked a series of odd jobs for spending money: as a clerk at Whitney Chemists, a drugstore near Washington Square; at an exotic plant shop, where I watered plants and made deliveries throughout Manhattan in a very cool Citroen station wagon; and at a head shop on Greenwich Avenue. I also ran a studio video camera once a week at WNYC, the public television station, in lower Manhattan. Through these interactions I began to feel a sense of belonging to the neighborhood community — no longer just passing through, but an actual resident.

In the two summers between my years at NYU, a documentary opportunity came my way. Back in California, our neighbor, Dr. Marvin Stark, was working with Project HOPE, an organization that brought healthcare services to underserved communities throughout the world.

Dr. Stark was Professor of Dentistry at University of California at San Francisco, and believed in building relationships and advocating peace through health. He bought a Greyhound bus and converted it into a dental office with three patient stations and recruited his dental students and fellow UCSF faculty to travel with him through California's Central Valley, treating migrant workers' children's teeth for free. He was a true advocate for social justice who understood that these hourly seasonal workers had no access to dental care.

As Dr. Stark describes it, he awoke one day to a thunderbolt: "I'm Jewish," he said to himself. "Why aren't I doing this in Israel?"

With that, he bought, equipped, and shipped a second bus to Tel Aviv, where he began treating Arab, Druze, and Jewish children throughout the Jewish state. Dr. Stark knew I was in film school and looking for opportunities to advance my career. He carefully crafted an offer for me to create a documentary about his Israel venture.

I followed Dr. Stark to Israel and began filming his every activity. The result was a film called, *Aliyah*, which translates from Hebrew as "ascension," and has also become the term used when Diaspora Jews make the permanent move to Israel. The film won the Council on International Nontheatrical Events (CINE) Award for Best Documentary.

The film was helpful in raising money for Dr. Stark's efforts, and I returned to Israel the following summer to do a follow-up documentary on his work. This time I brought Alice with me to engineer the sound.

It was there, in Israel, several years after we met and began working together that we fell in love.

Michael's family lived in Atlanta. After graduation we headed there, and, building on our credibility from *Aliyah*, pitched a documentary to the governor of the state, a young Jimmy Carter.

Through Michael's family, we had learned about a progressive center for developmentally disabled adults supported by Governor Carter and his wife, Rosalynn. The Georgia Center for the intellectually challenged was a facility without locked gates and doors, where clients were free to move inside and out of their own volition. There was no segregation of Blacks and Whites — almost unheard of in the South at that time — and it was also staffed by Blacks and Whites working side by side. It was a model for the country — the antithesis of what one might expect of an institution caring for people with the most serious challenges who cannot speak up for themselves. The Carters agreed that a documentary would be an excellent way to showcase the progressive work in mental health being accomplished under their leadership.

Governor Carter commissioned our project, and he worked closely with us, showing up at the public television studios where we edited our work. For four recent college graduates, it was an auspicious start to what we hoped would be lucrative film careers. We were living our passion, telling important stories, and having a ball.

It took us a year to make the documentary and when we were done, the one-hour program aired on PBS.

Hollywood

By then, it was clear to me that Atlanta was not a place where I could flourish as a filmmaker. Most of

ALICE ERBER AND HER HUSBAND, THE AUTHOR, AT THEIR WEDDING AT THE ATLANTIC CITY COUNTRY CLUB, 1978.

the people we met were hospitable and gracious in that Southern way, but just as with the East Coast, the South was not a place I could call home. I began to realize that I was not going to be able to make a living I aspired to doing documentary films. I had to make a radical break. The only viable alternative that I could imagine was a move to Hollywood.

Try as I might, my network and family connections did not extend to the Hollywood elite. Gaining acceptance into the Directors Guild required a sponsor; I came up short several times. There was a basic Catch-22: you had to be able to demonstrate guild-level work to gain admission, but you could not do guild-level work without guild membership. Going from meeting to meeting with a box of my film reels, each one a labor-of-love documentary, felt a little like my brief and humbling high-school experience going door-to-door as a Fuller Brush salesman. As familiar as I was with rejection, it stung that no one I met in Hollywood was interested in documentaries, and although I secured letters of recommendation in support of my application to the Directors Guild it wasn't enough.

I was becoming more and more despondent, recognizing that once again I was finding myself in yet another situation that was not a good fit. I had no connections in a town built on connections. My passion was documentary, not entertainment. I was lonely and out of step.

I finally got a job as a gofer at Filmways Pictures, whose market focus was night-of-the-week, made-for-TV movies. Soon I was learning the basic producing functions: scouting locations, managing logistics, and setting schedules. At this, it turns out, I had some ability. I quickly worked my way up to the position of assistant producer. One day a senior producer tapped me on the shoulder and told me, "You've made it, kid! You're going to be a big producer! You're going to live in Beverly Hills and drive a Mercedes-Benz!"

The trouble was, when I looked at all the guys putting the deals together and living in Beverly Hills, I realized they did not match my definition of success. I was much more drawn to the creative side, despite the ruthlessness I saw: if a director was late to the set even once, he was replaced. The entire industry felt cut-throat and vicious. As much as I loved making documentaries, I soon saw that Hollywood filmmaking was not a viable profession for me in the long term.

Now what? Here I was, with a Bachelor of Fine Arts degree in motion picture and television, living a life far different than the one I wanted, with little prospect for a course-correction into creative work.

Reversing the Path of Eisenstein and D. W. Griffith

My disillusionment with the film industry opened the door for Goody to ask me to reconsider whether architecture might be the right profession for me.

As a discipline, architecture offered a methodology for thinking and solving problems that greatly appealed to me. Growing up with Goody, often being in the office, watching projects evolve from the client's first vague thoughts to the eventual finished work, I had almost without knowing it imbibed much of my father's way of thinking. Goody's systematic way of assessing risk and reward, as well as the framework he utilized to evaluate trade-offs, provided me with a system for how to think about challenges. Like filmmaking, architecture is a creative endeavor. Persuasive to me was the fact that the father of film in Russia (Sergei Eisenstein) and the father of film in the United States (D. W. Griffith, *The Birth of a Nation*, 1915) both trained as architects. Somehow, it felt that a pivot to architecture was not such a far-fetched idea. But, if I chose it, becoming an architect would be years away.

Not yet convinced that I would ever go into practice, but lacking any other plan, I enrolled on the three-year graduate program in architecture at the University of California, Berkeley. The program was designed for people with undergraduate degrees, not in architecture but of diverse backgrounds, and in my class of 35 students were a priest, a teacher, a contractor, and an interior designer. As we formed into teams, our diversity provided each of us with what would become one of our most important lessons.

Consistent with my training at NYU, I came to believe that memorable storytelling is as fundamental in architecture as it is in film. I felt deeply that design involves the human spirit, the evolution of character, and the development of relationships between individuals. The program at Berkeley emphasized architecture as a social art. I liked the idea of creating environments that affect how people relate to one another. The approach fitted well with my deep commitment to fulfill the Jewish imperative to repair the world, *tikkun olam*. Making things better resonated deeply with my world view as it had evolved in the turbulent 1960s.

In my first year, I took a design studio from Professor Ray Lifchez called the *Social and Psychological Factors as Determinants of Architectural Form*. The class intended for the students first to be able to recognize their own values and assumptions, and then become sensitive to other people who might hold completely different values and assumptions. The idea was to imbed in us a profound sense of modesty about our own sense of 'rightness' and to foster empathy in us for all future users of the environment we would be shaping.

The actual work in the class was to create a living environment for a diverse collection of unrelated individuals that included opportunities to live, work, and play while accommodating privacy, individuality, and communal interaction. Working in teams, we built models that were 3 feet tall by 10 feet long, which resembled adult play houses. Interior surfaces were covered with magazine images, fabrics, and

THE AUTHOR, LEFT, WITH FELLOW ARCHITECTURE STUDENT MIKE SMITH, WITH THEIR FINAL PROJECT AT THE COLLEGE OF ENVIRONMENTAL DESIGN, UNIVERSITY OF CALIFORNIA AT BERKELEY.

wall coverings that precisely addressed the character, wants, and needs of our scripted users. Miniature-sized furniture and dollhouse light fixtures completed each "complex."

The level of thought, detail, and description that the students offered for each space was extraordinary. At the semester's end, during the final presentations of the projects, the connection between designer and user was both intimate and comprehensive. The experience left a memory etched within me: great design not only requires in-depth understanding of a building's users, but also empathy for their challenges and optimism that speaks to their aspirations.

I had experienced an epiphany: sculpting space has the power to shape life. I was so excited about the work that I volunteered to assist Professor Lifchez for each of the next two semesters as a teaching assistant.

In an equally memorable exercise, my teachers Sam Davis, Cathy Simon, and Bob Herman instructed us to come up with a three-dimensional cardboard module that was visually rich and highly refined in a form that was no larger than 12 by 12 by 12 inches. The next step was to put two of these modules together. Then we doubled the new double-module, so we were working with forms four times the size of the original, and so on. The design concept was to start

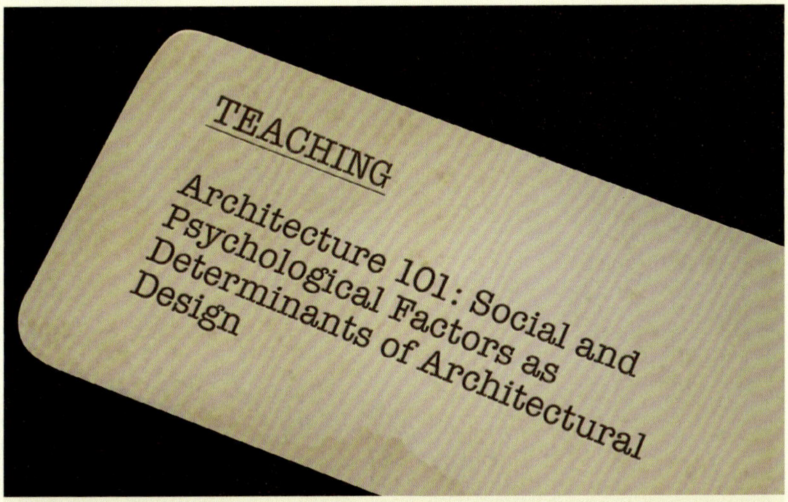

FROM TOP
THE ORIGINAL SYLLABUS FOR PROF. RAY LIFCHEZ'S COURSE.

BERKELEY STUDENTS REFINING SOME OF THE LARGE-SCALE MODELS.

ONE OF THE ELABORATE MODELS SHOWING THE HIGH LEVEL OF DETAIL.

OVERLEAF THE AUTHOR, SELF-PORTRAIT, 1961.

with a well-proportioned, visually compelling module, and then use that base as a multiplier, connecting similar modules or combinations of modules to create a harmonious and ordered assembly that enclosed a volume or "free space" created by virtue of the repeated forms.

I am particularly attracted to powerful ideas that can be choreographed into coherent stories that feel intuitive and effortless. These were among the big influences I took away from Berkeley, and, combined with all I learned from my father, provided the foundation on which I would refine my own ideas about what architecture would need to be in the coming decades.

One day when I was ten and taking art classes, I was given the task of making a watercolor self-portrait. I was given a palette limited to a few somber blues, plus white and black. I posed myself with my hands folded in a neat, dovetailed joint, hiding my mouth. My hair, in dramatic blocks of blue, occupied most of the top half of the picture, and the hairline across my forehead created a jagged edge that would have sufficed for a mountain range. The irises of my eyes were two huge black semicircles, floating over the only white used on the page. The feeling it conveyed was of a very serious young man, seeming to peer right through the viewer and on into the decades to come.

When we were gathered at dinner that night, with some trepidation as always, I presented my self-portrait in answer to Goody's regular query as to what I had achieved that day. He looked at it carefully, his expression barely showing whether or not he thought much of it. And then he gave his judgment.

"You can be an architect."

ROBBIE STEINBERG

9 REALITIES

1 ARCHITECTURE IS THE PURSUIT OF PERFECTION

Architecture strives to be the perfect embodiment of an idea as free as possible from all flaws or defects. It requires a process of methodical and relentless refinement.

MARKET STREET PARKING GARAGE	
Location	San Jose, California
Latitude/Longitude	37°20'12.0"N 121°53'37.7"W
Client	City of San Jose, California
Date	1982–86
Size	250,000 sq ft

THE GARAGE THAT COULD

In architecture, I believe collaboration can move us toward perfection.

One might not think of a parking garage as the most interesting place to begin a journey about architecture, community, and beauty. However, in the story of my life sculpting space, that's where it began. If you have been in downtown San Jose, you've probably seen it: five stories high, draped in a steel lattice, subtly tiled. That parking garage became the catalyst for the transformation of a city that had lost its heart and wanted desperately to find it and get it beating again.

San Jose grew and sprawled in the 1960s: the city hubs drifted to the periphery, and the downtown fell into disrepair, disinvestment, and despair. Even City Hall was moved to an outlying area. The formerly vibrant and thriving downtown core of California's first city, and second state capital, was near death.

Mayor Janet Gray Hayes, who ran on a campaign of "Let's make San Jose better before we make it bigger" in the mid-1970s, advocated smart growth in urban planning. She also touched our family by attracting women into government. My mother, Gerry Steinberg, became Santa Clara County's first female Supervisor and took on a leadership role in the preservation of the area's green foothills.

The next mayor, Tom McEnery, was driven to rebuild a viable downtown and stimulate economic development. To achieve his vision, he recruited Frank Taylor as Director of a new Redevelopment Agency. Taylor believed that redevelopment programs needed to be decisive, risk-taking ventures. He led a bond measure to fund revitalization work in the downtown, ultimately reaching $2 billion.

Taylor's strategy was to attract commercial office development that would bring business to downtown and generate a tax base to support the city. To compete with suburban-style office parks, which provided free parking, Taylor knew that he would have to neutralize the burden posed by paid parking downtown.

This was the background when we learned that among its first projects, the Redevelopment Agency planned to expand the Market Street garage, a two-story concrete mass that extended two blocks along San Pedro Square. The square comprised small-scale, historic buildings filled with eateries and shops — a significant downtown restaurant district that would also be expanding under the redevelopment plan. On the other side of the massive garage, central downtown constituted a collection of vacant building sites appropriate for new office development that would depend on the availability of additional parking.

Erected in the 1960s, the unattractive, two-story, poured-in-place concrete garage had one redeeming quality: it was structurally designed for a future expansion of up to two additional floors of parking. Nothing fancy was required. The obvious way to meet the city's requirement was to utilize the existing structural system and simply pour more concrete. Likely the job would go to the lowest bidder.

We felt well positioned to check off most of the boxes when the city issued its Request For a Proposal. Known as the go-to architect for San Jose civic projects, we had designed well-received, if smaller-scale, public buildings including libraries and community centers. Goody had developed close ties with Mayor

McEnery and Director Taylor, and I had forged a good relationship with Tom Aidala, the Redevelopment Agency's principal architect, who, like me, was a graduate of UC Berkeley's architecture program. The one box we could not check off was experience designing free-standing parking structures.

To mitigate our firm's weakness, we needed to partner with the right structural engineer. After conducting a bit of research on public garage specialists, I identified Cygna, based in San Francisco and headed by Sandy Tandowsky, as an attractive project partner. Cygna was a leader in parking structures and Tandowsky had worked previously with Aidala. A phone call, plus a bit of cajoling, convinced Tandowsky to join us in our quest to win the Market Street garage project.

Over Italian lunches that included a nice glass or two of wine, Tandowsky and I worked to persuade Tom that we were the right team for the job. We shared thoughts about design, urban planning, art, and literature. I looked for common touch points to build a relationship and help Tom feel comfortable that we were a good fit for the project.

Tom shared my architectural education background as well as my modern aesthetic. But Tom had become a formidable gatekeeper: he had been an active leader in San Francisco's 1971 urban design plan, which shaped the city for the next several decades. His gruff personality and tough demands put off developers and architectural consultants alike, so much so that architect Jon Jerde likened the San Jose redevelopment process to "trying to work with the Gestapo." When Adobe Systems came to downtown San Jose in the 1990s, it set as a condition that Tom would not be involved in designing its Park Avenue headquarters.

Yet involvement in the Redevelopment Agency projects' design process was exactly what Tom wanted. The Market Street garage was the first project up, and stakes were high to prove that public dollars were being deployed effectively. So as part of our strategy to win the RFP, Tandowsky and I agreed that we would include Tom in the design process. Little did we know what that would mean.

Over one of our lunches with Tom, our ears pricked up when he asked offhandedly, "Have you checked to see how many levels that garage will actually take?" What could he mean? The vision was to add two floors of concrete on the existing two floors of concrete.

One could easily imagine that there is not a lot of design opportunity in enlarging a city parking garage. And the existing vision did not really seem to offer much of one. We were not all that eager to be responsible for dumping a four-story concrete block adjacent to a small-scale, historic district. As passionate members of the San Jose community, we felt building such a beast would dissuade the caliber of potential developers the city wanted to attract to the downtown.

We began to explore options. Ideally, the garage expansion would go beyond standard issues of parking efficiency, ease of entry and exit, wayfinding, and security to lift the spirit of a depressed area and act as a catalyst for big dreams by young, new civic leadership.

Typically, once a structural system is designed and implemented — especially with a garage — it's very complicated to change it. Still, we considered alternative, more visually appealing approaches. And then we made the discovery that Tom had hinted at: by using steel instead of heavy, poured concrete, we could add an additional floor, providing fifty percent more

THE EXISTING POURED-IN-PLACE CONCRETE GARAGE.

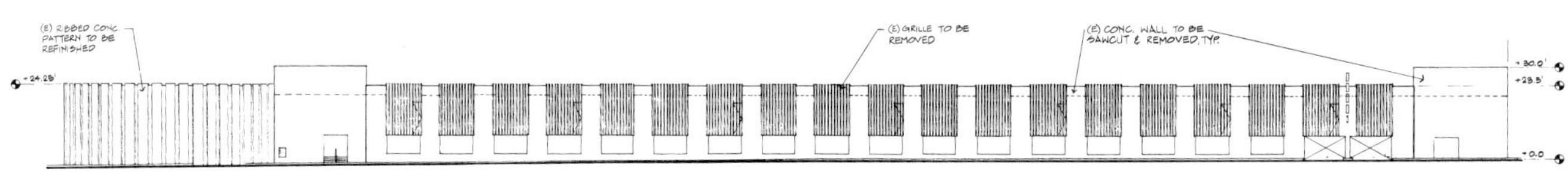

SAN PEDRO STREET – WEST ELEVATION (EXISTING)

1/16" : 1' – 0"

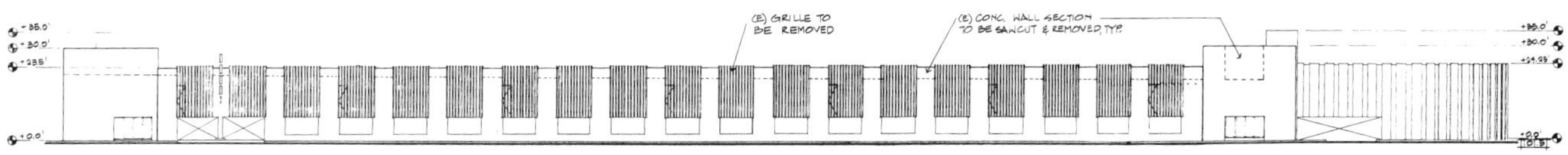

MARKET STREET - EAST ELEVATION (EXISTING)

1/16" : 1' - 0"

THE SITE PLAN SHOWS THE GARAGE'S FOOTPRINT: ONE BLOCK WIDE BY TWO BLOCKS LONG.

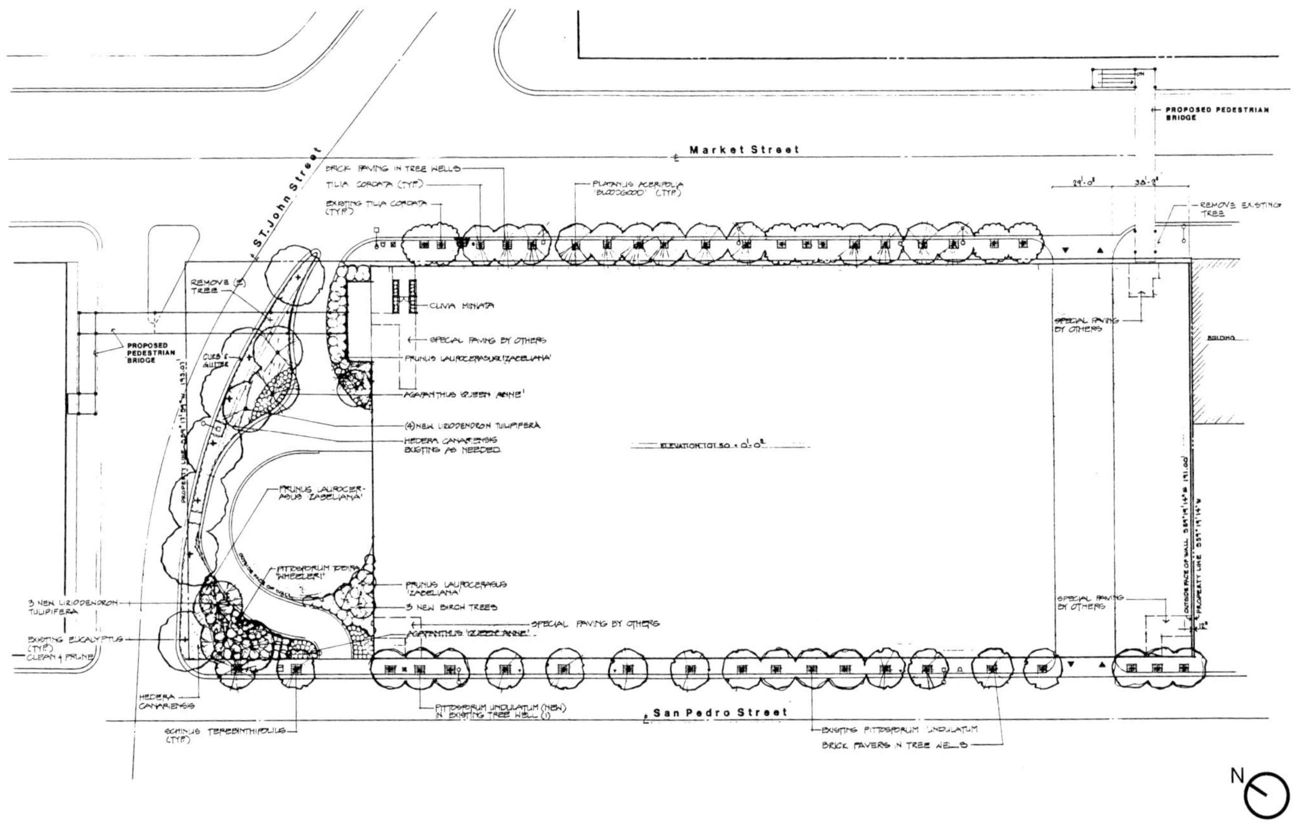

SITE PLAN

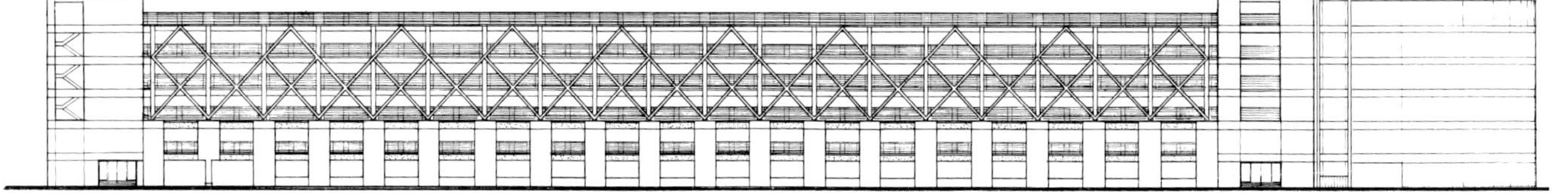

MARKET STREET ELEVATION (PROPOSED)

ONE OF THE MANY ITERATIONS, EACH REQUIRING SEVERAL DAYS OF DRAWING

parking than the RFP mandate. This novel approach surprised and exceeded the city's expectations. We presented this idea at our interview and learned that we were the only team with this solution. All the other applicants had based their bids on two more floors of poured concrete, which would have resulted in the eyesore we feared.

We won the job, and my role was to draw up the designs proposed by my father and Tom. Both, in their own way, shared a passion for pursuing perfection. Tom unapologetically tried to compensate for the unremarkable architecture in the downtown by creating something in his preferred aesthetic, heavily influenced by modernist Bauhaus architect Walter Gropius. Goody's approach, strongly impacted by a later Bauhaus giant Ludwig Mies van der Rohe, was driven by significantly different values. Instead of replicating designs for the masses, Goody preferred customization; instead of standardization, Goody preferred the unique. And instead of Tom's advocacy for a purely functional building, absent of adornment, Goody was concerned with proportion, intersections, and, as Mies had famously said, "God is in the details."

Being between the two of them, I wanted to somehow get the best out of both.

There were no computers in the early 1980s. I drew everything by hand. It could take me several days to draw a two-block-long building that was acceptable to both Tom and Goody. No sooner had I finished a draft then Tom would come by the next morning and suggest changes. I would go to work. Halfway through the revisions, in the early afternoon, Goody would come by and pull me in another direction. I was the fulcrum in a seesaw that balanced two opposing wings of the Bauhaus — my father on one end, and Tom, our increasingly difficult client, on the other. My job was to attempt to integrate these continuous revisions with what had already been done, so that instead of obliterating each other's work, each revision became a refinement.

Through this arduous process, I learned a great deal about the craft of architecture. I began to understand the importance of a building expressing a base, middle, and top. I learned that the base of an urban building needs to be made of permanent, maintenance-free materials that connect the building to the ground. The middle section could be more subdued, while the top and how the building meets the sky is, in many cases, how people recall a building. Goody and Tom taught me to look at the macro: the geometry of intersections entailed not only a connection at a column, but also the intersection

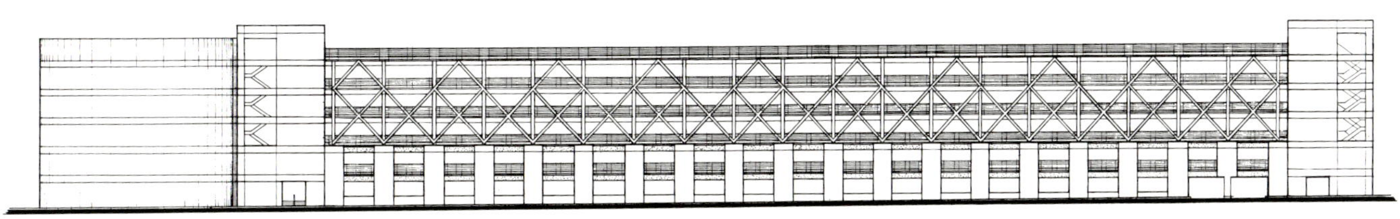

SAN PEDRO STREET ELEVATION (PROPOSED)

of the diagonal, steel cross-bracing as it met each of the three new horizontal parking levels. And they taught me to consider the micro: should the tiles be set in a running bond, herringbone, or basket-weave pattern? Very importantly, how do you handle a variation in the system, when a pattern is interrupted by a one-off condition like a vehicle entry or exit, for example? The details of the basket-weave tile pattern we selected were more static, and maximized the contrast with the dynamic steel cross-braced, diagonal new structure.

My father liked to say, "Any architect can draw a straight line. The way you evaluate the quality of an architect is how they manage intersections."

OPPOSITE NATURAL LIGHT PLAYS ACROSS THE BUILDING DURING THE DAY. LARGE OPENINGS THROUGHOUT MAXIMIZE VISIBILITY FROM THE STREET TO PROVIDE A SENSE OF SAFETY.

ABOVE AT NIGHT, AT THE HEART OF THE ENTERTAINMENT DISTRICT, THE STRUCTURE BECOMES ITS OWN MARQUEE.

So we refined, and refined, and refined. We considered the change in the building's appearance as the natural light shifted from morning, to midday, to night. Both Tom and Goody were focused, passionate designers who taught me that good architecture comes from refinement after refinement after refinement.

Ultimately, the Market Street garage addition was both utilitarian and visually appealing. The steel-braced frame exterior construction utilizes a diamond-patterned structure stacked on top of the concrete base. In a palette of gray and white tiles, it is graceful and playful — a whimsical latticework art piece conveying the happening vibe consistent with the Mayor's vision for San Jose's downtown. Today, decades later, San Pedro Square is the most active entertainment area in town, comprising pedestrian paseos filled with eateries and shops of all kinds.

At the time, the garage expansion was quite controversial. The design we implemented was hard for people to understand, in sharp contrast to the rest of downtown's utilitarian architecture. One of Tom's most frequent admonitions to any potential downtown developer was, "There will not be another mansard roof built in downtown San Jose." Our design was a far cry from the traditional roof of four sloping sides. Yet developers and the media, including some folks at the mansard-roofed Mercury News a few blocks away, persisted in asking, "Why can't you build something like we're used to?"

With the support of Tom, Frank Taylor, and Mayor McEnery, the garage was a statement that times were changing in San Jose, that there was a youthful new guard in town, willing to take risks. It was an invitation to developers and builders to come join us. This new direction was the incentive that enticed Adobe Systems to move its headquarters to downtown San Jose, becoming an anchor as well as a symbol for future development.

When we worked on the Market Street garage project in 1984, I proposed one addition to the design that the client had not originally called to include. It was an enhancement that removed one row of parking spots along San Pedro Street to create a line of mini shops behind roll-up doors that concealed the parked cars behind and enhanced the pedestrian experience by mirroring the retail activity across the street. Unfortunately, the project funds were not sufficient to implement both the garage expansion and the street-front reconfiguration.

Over thirty years later, in 2018, the community recognized the value of the San Pedro Historic District and came up with the money to implement the retail marketplace into the garage, precisely as we had recommended. The conversion of the east side of San Pedro Street from a pedestrian "dead zone" to retail paseo has improved the vitality and walkability of the district. Today, the weekly farmers' market, activated by shops on either side of the street, is one of the liveliest regular community gatherings in the city.

And with the completion of the mini shops, our vision for what perfection might be was ultimately realized.

THE BASKET-WEAVE TILE PATTERN, WITHOUT ANY DIAGONALS, PROVIDES CONTRAST WITH THE DIAGONAL STEEL STRUCTURE.

M
O
M
MOMENT

THIRTY-FOUR YEARS AFTER THE PROJECT'S START, THE STREET LEVEL FINALLY CAME ALIVE WITH SHOPS AND PEDESTRIAN LIFE, COMPLETING THE INITIAL VISION.

2 ARCHITECTURE IS INHERENTLY DIS-RUPTIVE

Architecture doesn't exist in isolation. It is, in effect, like joining an existing conversation. Architecture should be responsive to its context, purpose, and moment in time.

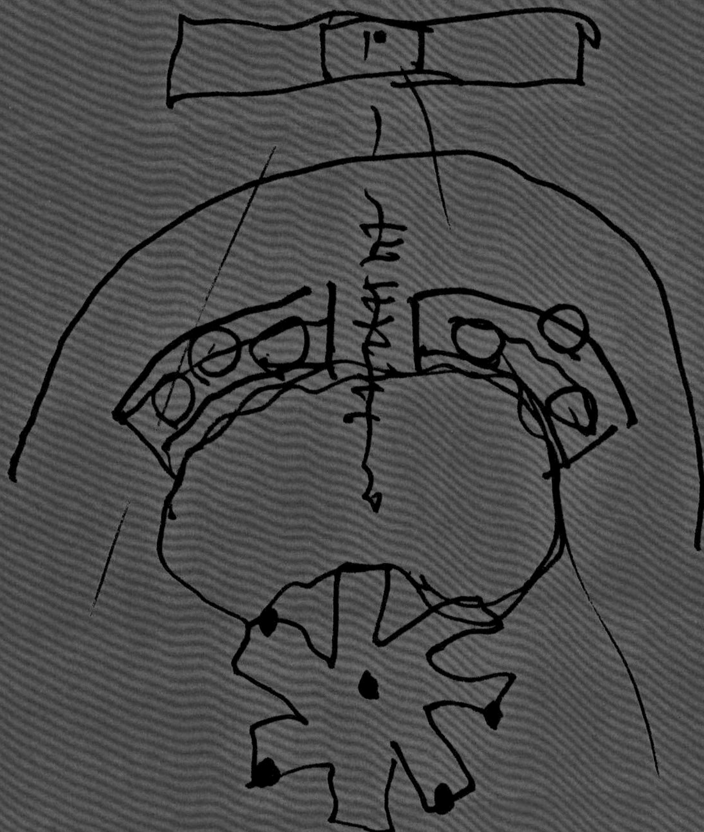

CAL POLY FACULTY OFFICE BUILDING

Location	San Luis Obispo, California
Latitude/Longitude	35°18'04.7"N 120°39'33.9"W
Client	State of California
Date	1987–92
Size	25,255 sq ft
Awards	American Institute of Architects, Award of Merit, 1991

A PLATFORM FOR REBELLION

I was sitting in my office puzzling over a remark made by one of my colleagues who, in reviewing our design for a custom house on a beautiful site with majestic oak trees, asked the following: "Which would be preferable? Should our design be compatible with what is already there, or would it be better to be disruptive?"

I was thinking that architecture is like walking into a room where a conversation is already taking place. A new building or development almost always takes place in an existing context of some kind. Our requirement, as disrupters, is to understand what has already been said, and then decide whether we're going to join in with the least amount of disruption, or whether we might redirect the conversation altogether.

I was jarred back into the present when my phone rang.

"Is this Robert Steinberg?" a voice asked.

"Yes, it is," I replied.

"Well, Mr. Steinberg, this is your lucky day."

Usually I would just hang up. But I hesitated. "Who is this?"

CAL POLY

The caller explained that, without even so much as a single interview, our firm had been awarded the commission to design a faculty office expansion at California Polytechnic State University (Cal Poly) in San Luis Obispo. Unbeknownst to me, among the many institutional RFPs that our new marketing manager had completed, was one for the California State University system. We had landed our firm's first higher-education project.

Once I realized that the call was no joke, I was elated by this opportunity for growth, change, and expansion into a new market, working with a government client on a highly competitive project that had the potential to bring the firm prestige and visibility beyond our local work.

I also had a bit of fear. A state government project in San Luis Obispo — a three-hour drive away — lay a little outside my comfort zone. Most of my clients were local, private clients with whom I met face-to-face and developed relationships. This was a project that would entail a by-the-book, formal process that would be new to me.

On the plus side, I knew the layout and vibe of the Cal Poly campus: I had often visited my best friend there when he was a student in the early 1970s. My memories of San Luis Obispo swarmed back — "California Dreamin," the parties, waking up on the beach at sunrise. I looked forward to seeing it again through fresh eyes.

The architect's job is not only to manage the client's budget, but also the firm's budget. We knew the Cal State project fees were modest, so our budget to deliver the work would have to be modest, too. We also wanted to have the time to observe campus activities, including circulation patterns, surges between class periods, and how students currently utilized outside spaces. Our challenge was to balance the time to design and produce the work in the office with time spent on site ensuring we understood the needs and desires of the client and building a relationship with them.

On our first visit to Cal Poly, our small team met with representatives from the Chancellor's and Dean's offices, the campus architect, and the facilities manager. The Cal Poly team explained that the project had been in the planning stage for years. University officials had put in countless hours and extensive efforts to rise to the top of the list of capital projects competing for California State University funding. They described in detail the need to expand faculty office capacity in the sciences, which were currently in a one-story, spiderlike, generic building: a central hub with eight legs, each housing a separate department — chemistry in one, physics in another, biology in a third, and so on.

Not only had the need for more offices been identified, but the project managers had also determined how to add them. They planned to extend each leg of the spider to add a couple of faculty offices for each department.

We listened respectfully to the staff's definition of the problem and the obvious, but inelegant, solution they were proposing.

That afternoon we walked the campus and thought about the challenge. We studied the site, including a sloping, oddly shaped remnant of land between the existing science building and the administration building, over which the university President enjoyed unobstructed views of the Pacific Ocean. We would soon learn that this view was not to be disrupted.

In our evaluation, the existing science building presented a host of troublesome potential issues. It was actually two buildings — one built in the 1950s and the other erected in the 1960s — with different mechanical systems, different floor levels, and different materials. The floorplan was a series of dead-ends; the front door was deeply recessed from the perimeter of the building and poorly marked, making it difficult to find entry.

TOP THE CAMPUS IS NESTLED IN A VALLEY WITHIN THE TOWN OF SAN LUIS OBISPO THAT LOOKS TOWARD THE PACIFIC OCEAN.

ABOVE ONE OF THE ORIGINAL WINGS OF THE SPIDER-LIKE BUILDING THAT THE CAL POLY TEAM WANTED US TO EXPAND.

The wings of the hub-and-spoke-shaped building had no connections between them, which precluded interdisciplinary interaction. Isolating the biology faculty from the chemistry faculty when biochemistry was an emerging and exciting field seemed counterproductive. The building's spokes had no connection to the outdoors either, limiting the types of activities that could be undertaken, but even more so,

should be responsive to its context, purpose, and moment in time.

depriving the occupants of the splendor of the campus's coastal setting. In addition, part of the campus circulation pattern cut right through the center of the building, further dividing it into separate north and south wings.

No matter what we might do to these buildings, they could never be showpieces for our practice. Why take on this project without the potential of leveraging it for other higher-education opportunities?

On our very first visit, we quickly recognized that the proposed solution — making eight small additions to the older structures, each with a variety of field conditions — would not only be exceedingly expensive to build, but would also be highly disruptive to ongoing operations. It seemed to us that the project managers had failed to consider the cost, the schedule, and the level of disruption to campus life their solution entailed. Walking around the site, we became

RED CIRCLES SHOW THE LOCATIONS OF THE PROPOSED MULTIPLE ADDITIONS.

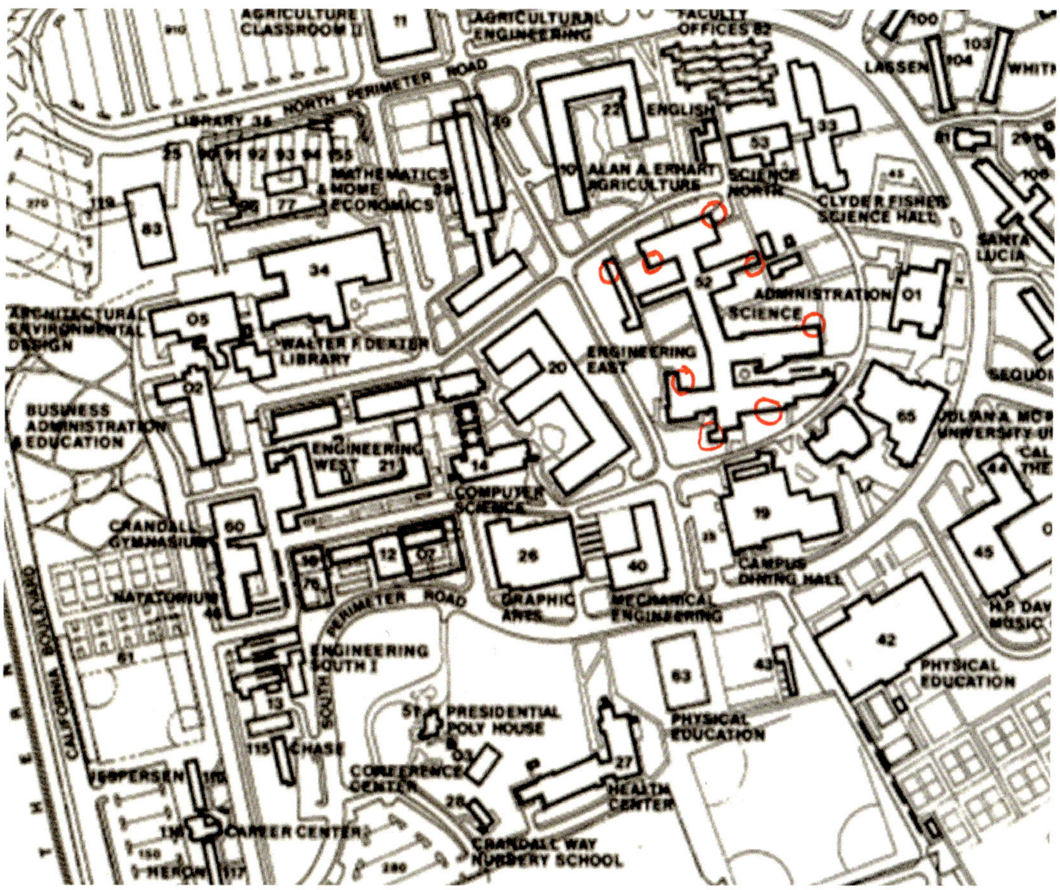

N

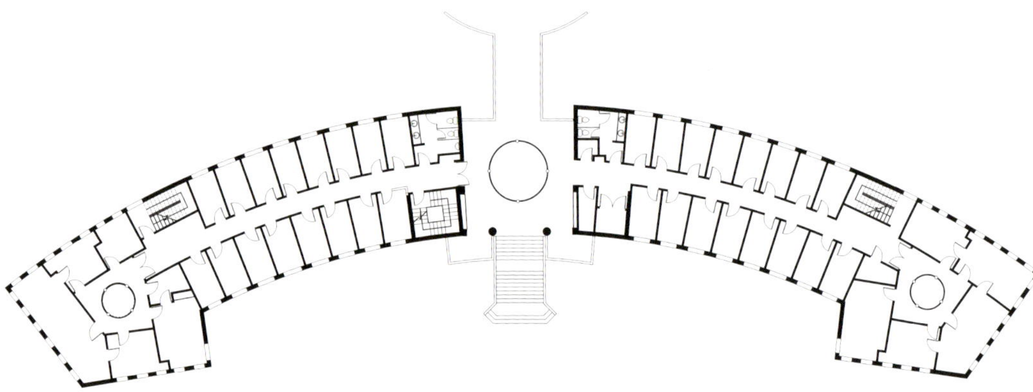

THE COMPLETED FACULTY OFFICE BUILDING DEFINES, FOR THE FIRST TIME, A SCIENCE QUADRANGLE.

THE SECOND-LEVEL FLOORPLAN SHOWS THE PUBLIC THRUWAY CROSSING THE FACULTY'S ARCING PATHS, WITH DEPARTMENT RESOURCE AREAS AT EACH CIRCULAR TERMINUS IN THE PENTANGLES.

convinced that what the client wanted could not be accomplished. It was more like an emergency graft, extending the life of something that was not very healthy in the first place.

In fact, we started to wonder if our "lucky day" phone call was the result of some other architect walking away from this seemingly impossible "solution" handed down by the project managers. What started out as elation over a great opportunity was now looking more like a potential nightmare.

Over the years, clients have asked me, is it better to remodel or build new? There is no simple, one-size-fits-all answer, but there are some consistent factors to consider.

With a remodel, the architect must assess each condition. Every time a horizontal and vertical surface intersects, a unique and different challenge is presented. Existing trims, fixtures, and fittings may no longer be available. Often, project drawings are incomplete or inaccurate: many times, changes made in the field are not recorded on the construction documents. Furthermore, during demolition, you sometimes discover that structural connections were not installed correctly, or you find dry rot or termites in a wall you have opened up, requiring mitigation. A remodel like this one, which included many small pieces, often requires more time and money than erecting new construction.

Aside from these pragmatic considerations were intangible values. Is the building historic? Does it hold sentimental attachment for its users? Are there installations within it, such as memorials or personal elements that cannot be replicated? Fortunately, none of these softer aspects were present.

Taking a step back, we pondered just what was the problem the university was trying to solve?

My partner, Ernie Yamane, and I walked up to the top of a hill between the science and administration buildings in silence. We turned and took in the beautiful view. We soon identified three key issues:

1 The proposal was really eight different projects, adding to each of the eight wings of the building. Would it be more efficient to hire one contractor to do each wing sequentially, creating a construction zone for years to come? Or would we hire eight contractors and do the additions all at once, effectively closing the building and dislocating its academic programs?
2 Our out-of-town location meant that our overseeing of day-to-day construction would be limited — a concern on a project that by state law mandated that we rely on the lowest-bid, cheapest local builder, regardless of quality or experience.
3 Assuming we could overcome all these constraints, what would the impact of the finished project be on students and faculty?

Architecture doesn't exist in isolation. It is, in effect, like joining an existing conversation. Architecture

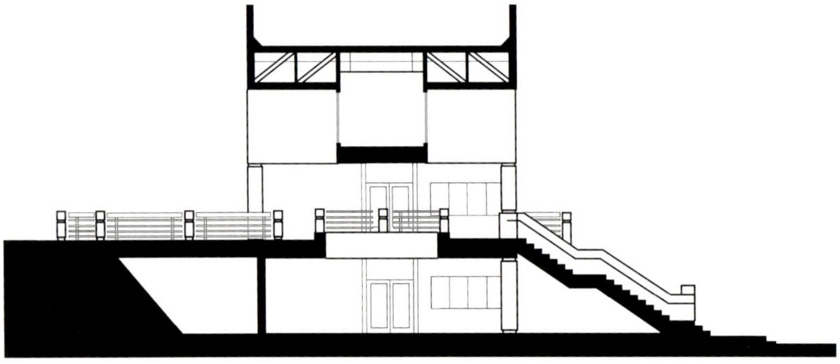

SECTION WITH THE STREET ON THE LEFT AND, ON THE RIGHT, STEPS TO THE QUAD LEVEL.

OPPOSITE THE OUTDOOR LOBBY. THE BUILDING WAS NOTCHED TO MINIMIZE THE FEELING OF COMPRESSION FROM THE THIRD FLOOR ABOVE.

BELOW DETAIL OF OUTDOOR LOBBY.

An architect is trained to solve more than functional challenges. We are taught that effective architecture builds community, raises the spirits, is disruptive, and possibly creates something beautiful that was not there before. The client's imagined solution did none of these things. It did not foster connection, it did not link indoors and outdoors, it did nothing to contribute to the broader campus community, and it certainly was not beautiful. In short, it was inconsistent with all of my training.

Ernie and I concluded that the proposed solution amounted to throwing good money after bad. If we agreed to serve as the architect of record, we were not going to make the client happy, and we faced losing a ton of money. We should have given serious consideration to walking away.

Unfortunately, that was not a possibility for me. My upbringing had branded me deeply with one overriding core belief: you do not quit. It never crossed my mind as an option.

The actual problem was that Cal Poly was growing and needed room for more faculty. Just sticking some spaces on the ends of the existing buildings would barely solve the problem in the short term, but it would return in a few years.

And in that moment, we had a radical vision.

Instead of a remodel, we decided that Cal Poly needed a new faculty building. And we knew where it needed to go: unfortunately, right in front of the President's cherished view.

We envisioned a new, free-standing, three-story building to the east of the existing complex. It would be curved, to follow the road that defined the edge of the space. The entire science faculty would be able to reside together, fostering greater interdisciplinary interaction. The building would sculpt a new outdoor classroom/amphitheater/social space between the two existing buildings, which would be used for class activities, science experiments, and even commencement exercises each spring. In defining this space, the building would create a science "quadrangle" of sorts, turning a shapeless outdoor area into a statement of the importance of the basic sciences. And without a drawn-out construction process that would wreak havoc for years, the new construction would be separate from ongoing operations.

We thought about

Archite
in isola
like jo
convers
shoul
its con
m

how the building could best enhance student and faculty interaction. The interior would be organized much like a shopping mall, with anchor activity drawing users to either end of the building, and smaller-scale elements in between them feeding off the circulation. We proposed an arcing dumbbell-shaped structure, with stairs and restrooms at one end and collaborative workspaces at the other. Individual faculty offices would line each side of the corridor, ensuring random hallway interactions as faculty made their way to the end of the hall to use the restrooms, visit the administrative offices, or meet colleagues in dedicated meeting rooms.

With modest-sized offices, the building itself would be quite narrow, affording it the opportunity to take advantage of the ocean breeze for natural ventilation. To that end, we included operable, transom windows over each door to facilitate airflow and add natural light and openness to the design aesthetic. We maximized glass in the door panels to allow light to flow into the corridors — the transparency would provide an invitation to students to drop in. Unlike the existing building, with its multiple circulation routes terminating in dead-ends, the new building's hallways terminated at loops that encouraged free-flowing movement. Supplementing the horizontal connections, we designed a vertical space stretching up through all three floors to provide a visual connection between departments housed on different levels. An oversized skylight atop the space flooded the building with even more natural light.

The design would convert disorganization into coherence. Our visual wayfinding system would ensure the students found faculty offices more easily. By enclosing a large space, we would create an outdoor "room." And, by creating a coherent mini-campus, the new building would increase the connection between the sciences and the larger campus community.

FROM THE STREET, THE BUILDING IS NOTCHED INTO THE HILL. FEW PEDESTRIAN VIEWS REVEAL ALL THREE STORIES AT ANY ONE TIME.

In addition to the variety of circulation options and spaces for congregating, we added two performance areas to the ceremonial stair. On either end of the second-level landing, we envisioned overlooks large enough for a table and chairs, or sufficient to conduct science experiments that could be launched from the second floor down to the terrace below. The lowest-level stair landing would be exaggerated and bowed outward to create a podium — a platform from which a student rabble-rouser, such as I had once been, would be able to deliver a speech if so inclined.

By the time we were done with our planning, the building was already alive for us. It was something we could walk through, imagine at various times of day and night, test changes, refine and refine. Now our challenge would be to convince the Cal Poly team to let go of their

TERRACING DOWN THE HILL: THE ADMINISTRATION BUILDING WITH THE PRESIDENT'S OFFICE (TOP LEFT); THE FACULTY OFFICE BUILDING WITH REDUCED HEIGHT OF EACH END PENTANGLE, AND THE BEGINNING OF THE QUAD ITSELF ON THE RIGHT.

exist
fect,
ing
cture
e to
and

old vision, and see what we saw. We put together a beautiful and complete presentation, delivered it to the team, and waited. The Cal Poly project team was quiet. Not in a good way.

"Prove it," they responded to our point-by-point assessment that our proposal provided a better long-term outcome.

And so, over time, we did. Each step of the way — from concept schematics, to design development, to construction documents — we filtered the plan against schedule, budget, and function. At each step, the stakeholders were presented with another opportunity to poke holes in the concept, trying to identify shortcomings that might emerge.

On one particularly memorable visit, to underscore their emphatic point that the view from the President's office must not be obstructed, project managers arranged for us to visit the office. It felt as though we were about to be terminated when the managers stood facing the view and reiterated previous directives. From there, we could see that our proposed three-story building would, in fact, impinge on the view. But all three stories were needed to meet the project specs. What to do? Suggest the President move his office? Spend more time on the roof?

We decided to lower the building. It would still be three stories, but we found a way to notch the building into the hill. Thus, the lowest level would be the same level as the existing buildings, the middle floor would sit at the elevation of the roadway, and the top level would be just one floor above ground level, thereby retaining the President's view.

We finally won approval, and construction began. Needing to lower the building ate into our budget, but, in the end, the new faculty office building was completed on time and within the original budget for the piecemeal solution, just as we had assured the project team it would be. For the same budget, the faculty office building added far more value than the university had anticipated with its original call for fragmented additions.

An American Institute of Architects' (AIA) Award was icing on the cake.

Now, many decades later, I came across Cal Poly's current master plan. I was surprised and delighted that our 1987 concept that had sculpted a kind of quad now had a name: the Centennial Green.

With that success, the building and the area that it transformed, had created a *new context* for all of Cal Poly, having an impact far greater than we initially could have imagined.

The new plan states: "The Centennial Green, located in the Science building area adjacent to the University Union, should be a key central space within the instructional core. It should not only function as the geographic and physical center of campus, but it should serve, along

229C
229D

OPPOSITE A DEPARTMENT RESOURCE LOOP, WITH GLAZED CONFERENCE ROOMS OFF IT, AND VERTICALLY OPEN TO OTHER LEVELS.

RIGHT GLASS FACULTY DOORS WITH TRANSOM WINDOWS ABOVE, BRING DAYLIGHT AND OCEAN BREEZES INTO THE BUILDING.

THE OVERLOOKS CREATE A POINT OF FOCUS FOR THE QUAD.

like joining an existing conversation. Architecture should be responsive to its context, purpose, and moment in time.

with the student union, as the social heart of the campus and as a central student gathering space."

Looking at the influence our project has had on the development of the Cal Poly campus, sculpting space that has reshaped campus life, I realized that the revolution I had imagined starting on the speaker's podium, was alive in the entire building. By unequivocally accepting the fact that anything we intended to do was going to be disruptive, we were in fact creating a new sense of community and healing the space. Architecture is inherently disruptive, and sometimes we need to let it be without apology. "Let the revolution begin!"

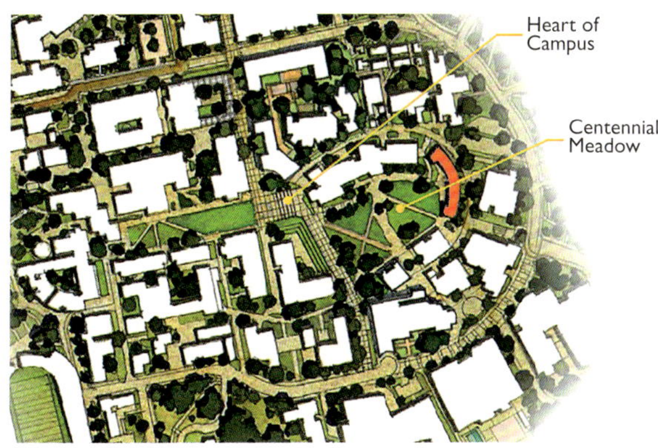

THE 2035 CAMPUS MASTER PLAN REVEALS HOW THE FACULTY OFFICE BUILDING CONTINUES TO SHAPE THE FUTURE OF THE CAMPUS.

THE VIEW FROM THE PRESIDENT'S TERRACE, PRESERVED

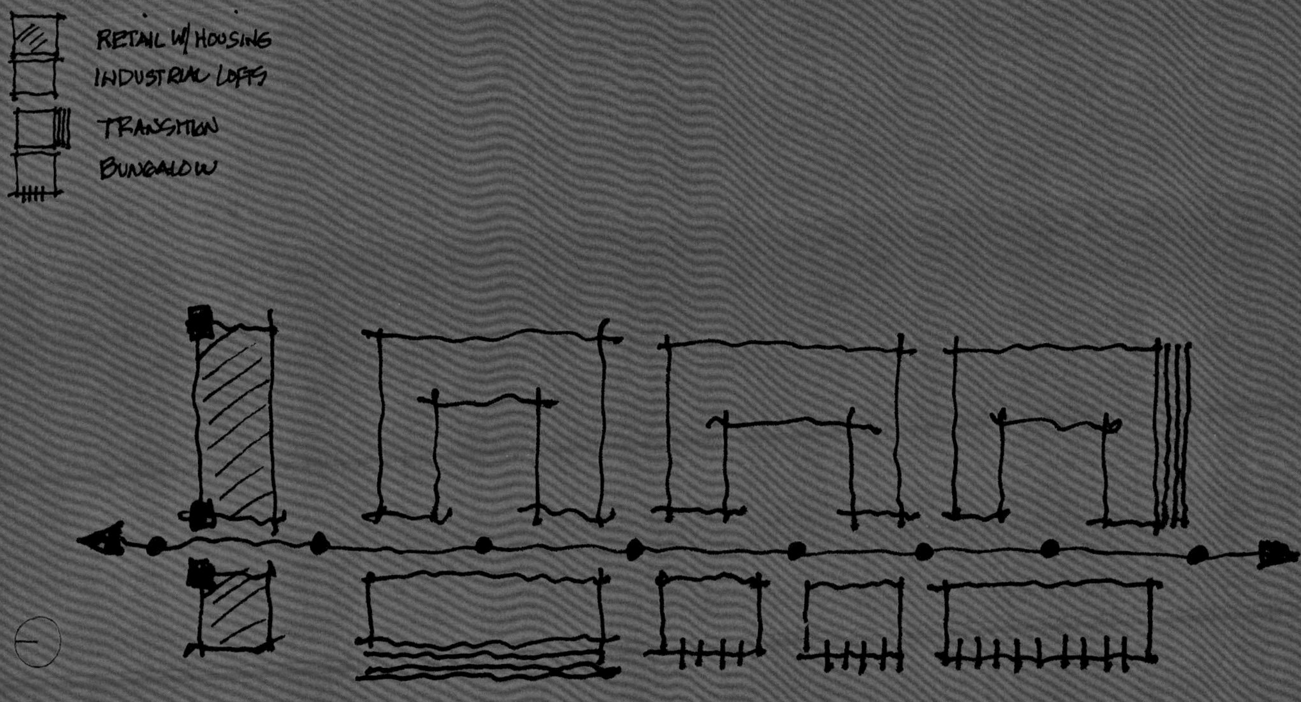

AVALON AT CAHILL

Location	San Jose, California
Latitude/Longitude	37°19'53.8"N 121°54'18.7"W
Client	Avalon Bay Communities
Date	1999–2003
Size	387,000 sq ft

THE POWER OF SMALL HARMONIES

Fortunately, not every project requires a revolution. Some developers advance perfectly acceptable frameworks in which the architect can practice their craft and add value to an already strong general direction.

The Avalon at Cahill in San Jose, a residential complex, was the opposite of a revolution. It did not require the rebellion and radical contradiction that Cal Poly did. Rather, the urban planner had laid out a compelling set of guidelines that were useful and suitable for the project.

In the late 1980s and early 1990s, the Midtown Specific Plan provided a vision for an area of San Jose that was undergoing considerable transition and change. Located immediately west of downtown, Midtown originally was part of the Rancho Los Coches Mexican land grant along the historic Alameda, in the heart of the fertile Santa Clara Valley, which supported livestock, wheat, dairy, and orchard farming. With the advent of rail transportation and the invention of refrigerated rail cars in the 1860s, Midtown became a thriving food-processing, packaging, and transshipment center. The proximity of the area to the fertile valley and fruit orchards made it a natural location for canneries, warehouses, and related industrial uses.

But by the 1950s, the historic role of Midtown as a food-processing, packaging, and transshipment center began to wane as urban development replaced the surrounding orchards, and interstate trucking eclipsed rail as the predominant mode of distribution.

Thirty years later, city planners were focused on Midtown infill development as a strategy to address housing shortages and stimulate downtown revitalization. Infill offers many benefits when compared with "greenfield" suburban development: it can reduce sprawl, revitalize downtowns and older neighborhoods, create more walkable, transit-oriented communities, reduce infrastructure expenses, and provide residents with a greater variety of housing options.

The Midtown Specific Plan encouraged coordinated development to create a new mixed-use community, including high-density housing oriented to transit, while maintaining some commercial and industrial uses.

Successful infill development requires a high level of sensitivity and finesse to appropriately respond to existing conditions and adjacencies — that is, to join the "conversation" already in place. Visiting the site, I did my utmost to assess the existing "conversation" and how best to respond to it. As I made my way around the site's perimeter, the shifting conversations were disjointed, disharmonious, and noisy. The long, narrow site on which the Avalon development was to take shape was surrounded by a different attribute on each of its four sides: canneries,

VIEWED TOWARD THE EAST: THE DIRIDON RAIL STATION; BEYOND, A FORTHCOMING GOOGLE CITY; AND THE SKYLINE OF DOWNTOWN SAN JOSE.

IMMEDIATELY TO THE EAST OF THE SITE, ONE OF THE ORIGINAL DEL MONTE CANNERIES.

retail, single-family housing, and a new park planned as part of the project. It was hard to derive a coherent sense of what this site might be trying to communicate.

Designing for the parcel in a way that was in harmony with each of its unique neighbors, we utilized four different strategies to make the new buildings fit comfortably into their context.

On the side facing the aged Del Monte warehouse, we erected large-scale, multi-storied buildings of corrugated metal, reflecting an industrial character to create a complementary scale and rhythm to the remaining cannery.

On The Alameda side of the site, we adopted the local customary form of housing above the retail, and introduced recycled brick and metal detailing to connect to the site's previous warehouses.

On the third side we created a transitional mode, replacing metal with plaster and introducing wood details, such as horizontal wooden trellises.

And, on the fourth side, where our development faced single-family bungalows, we designed two-story townhouses, each with their own covered front porch. Complete with picket-fence yards and covered porches, they were ideal for families, and seamlessly integrated into the existing neighborhood.

The all-important internal shared public realm of the project was defined by the interstitial space *between* the buildings. The spaces were as important and as impactful as the buildings themselves. We recognized that the space formed between the buildings facing Bush and Wilson streets was large enough to accommodate an on-site pedestrian artery running the length of the site. Like a circulation system that connects different parts of the body, this artery established a visual and experiential sequence of travel that connected the retail and public transportation services on The Alameda side of the site, past three neighborhoods with individual open spaces to eventually arrive at a new community park.

Today, the neighborhood and even the region around Avalon at Cahill is showing the effects of our efforts to catalyze, as opposed to disrupt. The park we developed as a new community amenity

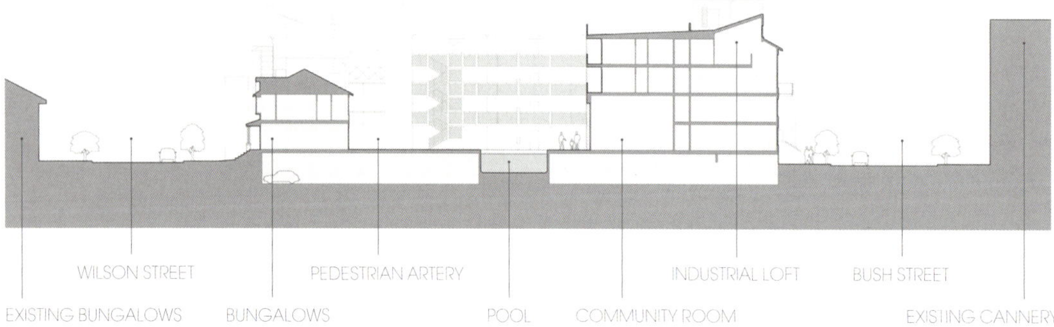

SECTION SHOWING, FROM LEFT TO RIGHT, EXISTING BUNGALOWS; WILSON STREET; HEIGHT-MATCHING BUNGALOWS; ONE OF THREE INTERNAL COURTYARDS; A TWO-STORY COMMUNITY ROOM AS PART OF A LOFT BUILDING; THE LOFTS THEMSELVES; AND THE EXISTING CANNERY ACROSS BUSH STREET (THE HEIGHT OF WHICH THE LOFTS MATCH).

CLOSEWISE FROM TOP LEFT SKETCHES OF THE INDUSTRIAL LOFTS; RETAIL STORES WITH HOUSING ABOVE; CRAFTSMAN-STYLE BUNGALOWS, AND A TRANSITIONAL BUILDING, FROM LOFT TO BUNGALOW, INTRODUCING WOOD DETAILS.

ABOVE AN INDUSTRIAL-STYLE LOFT BUILDING.

OPPOSITE TOP RETAIL STORES WITH RESIDENTIAL ABOVE.

OPPOSITE BELOW LEFT TRANSITION BUILDING AT CAHILL PARK.

OPPOSITE BELOW RIGHT CRAFTSMAN BUNGALOWS WITH TRADITIONAL STOOPS AND FRONT PORCHES.

TIME TO UNWIND
TIME FOR REFLECTION

PARKING ONLY

thrives. The entire area has continued to grow, with wonderful new restaurants, a Whole Foods across the street, and Google moving in next door, establishing a campus for 20,000 people and basically re-centering downtown San Jose. The adjacent rail hub will eventually become the equivalent of Grand Central for Northern California, bringing together BART (Bay Area Rapid Transit), and other regional rail systems, with Amtrak and high-speed rail that will connect to Northern and Southern California.

The most common, short-term solution to multi-family housing is to design one building and repeat it multiple times on a site. With Avalon at Cahill, such a solution would have deteriorated into repetitive dullness, leaving the impression that the project landed, fully formed on the site from some distant location. It would have initiated a path to continued impoverishment.

Instead, we attempted to be minimally disruptive, aspiring to gracefully enter the existing conversation. Each side of the development talks to its neighbors in a way that is compatible, and yet advances the Midtown district to include residential options in support of San Jose's Midtown Specific Plan. The project itself has become for the region the very definition of what an infill development ought to be.

THE CONTINUUM OF DISRUPTION

Architecture is inherently disruptive. Once we accept that, we can consciously decide the level of disruption necessary and appropriate for the community we are trying to shape. In the instance of Cal Poly, not being disruptive would have added to the formlessness that was already plaguing the science campus. By deliberately taking a bold view of what was possible, a new context was created that suddenly made the old buildings make some kind of sense, and the outdoor space that the new building defined quickly became the heart of the campus.

The opposite approach was appropriate for Avalon at Cahill. By addressing each of the disharmonious faces surrounding the project, small harmonies were brought to each of the four conversations, instilling a new sense of peace and place to the community. In this instance, the disruption was self-effacing, something that can be a little uncomfortable for architects.

And although Cal Poly was deliberately disruptive, and Avalon at Cahill was deliberately stealthy, both became transformative organizing forces in their communities.

OPPOSITE THE CANNERY-LIKE FEEL OF THE HOUSING OVER THE RETAIL, FROM THE REAR OF THE RETAIL STORES.

RIGHT SURFACES THAT MAY BE TOUCHED WERE GIVEN INCREASED REFINEMENT.

LEFT AVALON AT CAHILL, AT BOTTOM, WAS THE FIRST SAN JOSE URBAN INFILL PROJECT. THE SITE OF GOOGLE'S NEW CITY IS TO THE RIGHT OF THE WHITE-ROOFED SAP PAVILION, UPPER LEFT.

OPPOSITE AT THE FRONT, THE NEW UPSCALE RETAIL STREET. ON THE LEFT, BUSH STREET IS NARROWER AND MORE URBAN, FACED BY EQUALLY TALL BUILDINGS ON BOTH SIDES. ON THE RIGHT, A DOUBLE ROW OF TREES ON WILSON STREET STRENGTHENS THE MORE RESIDENTIAL FEEL; AND, AT THE TOP, THE NEW CAHILL PARK.

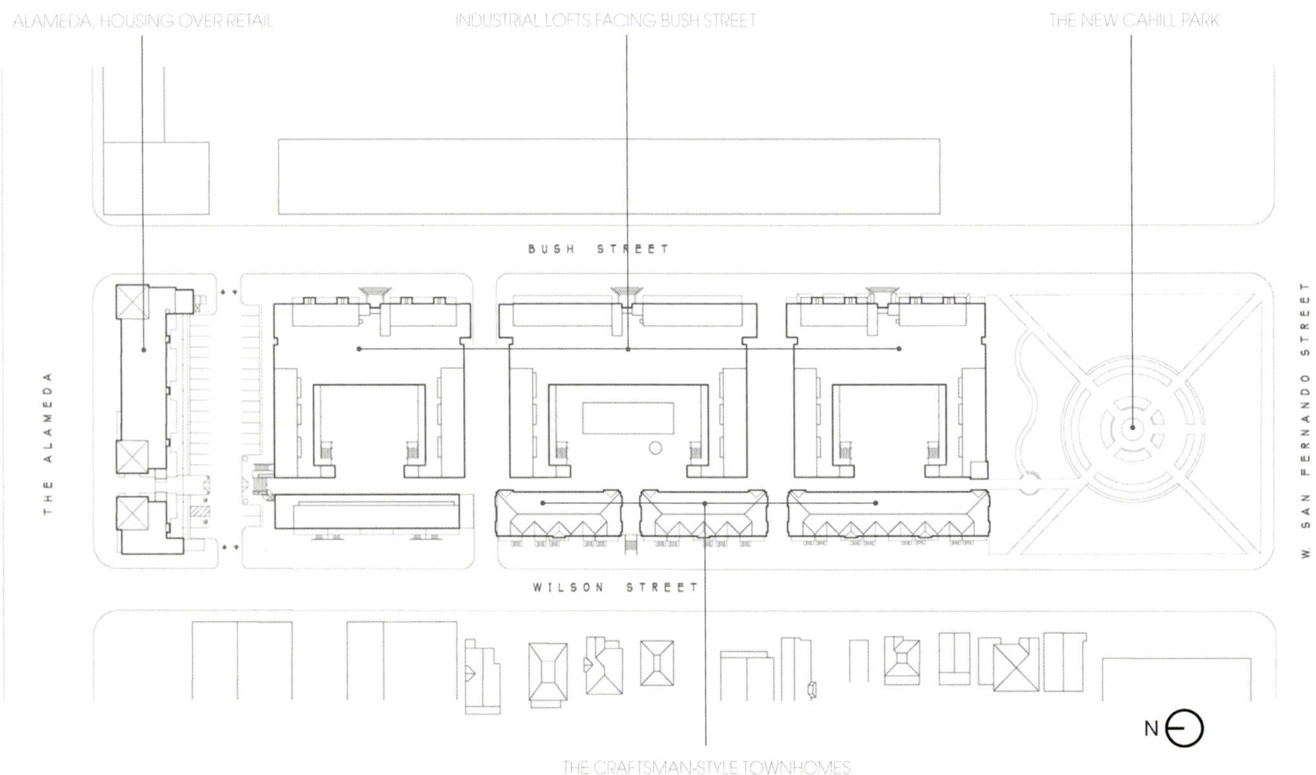

ARCHITECTURE BUILDS COMMUNITY

Architecture is a social art that choreographs human interacti(-_-)n.

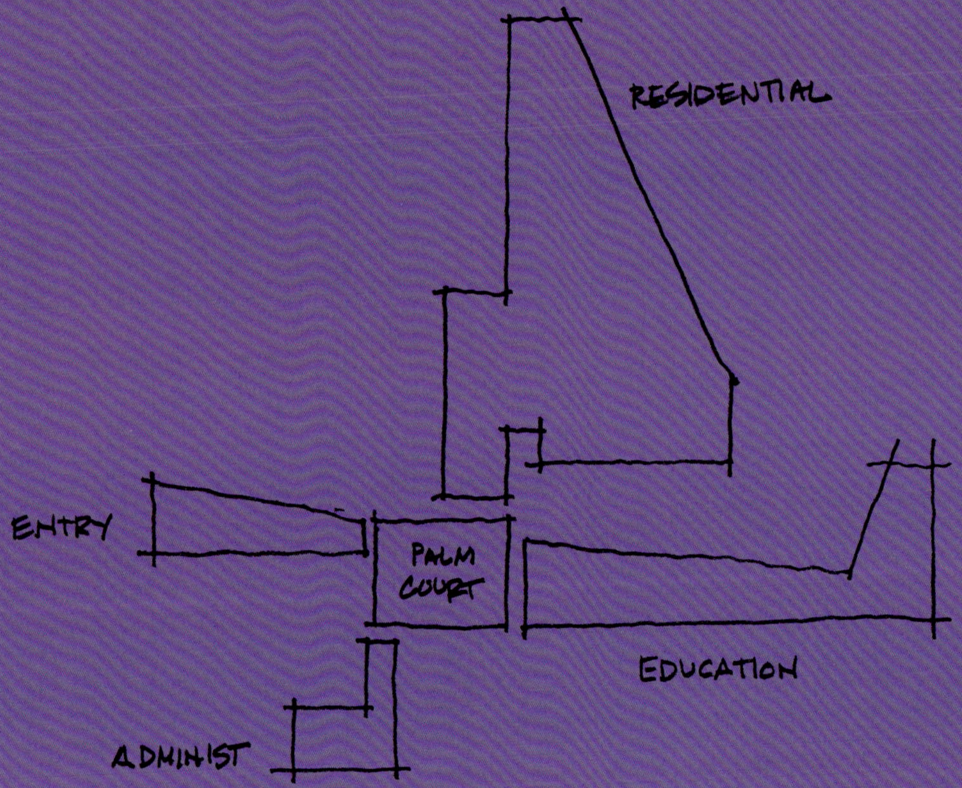

JOB CORPS CENTER	
Location	San Jose, California
Latitude/Longitude	37°22'00.6"N 121°49'14.9"W
Client	U.S. Department of Labor
Date	1990–95
Size	118,000 sq ft
Awards	American Institute of Architects, Award of Merit, 1995

TO BEND THE TRAJECTORY OF YOUNG LIVES

The Job Corps was founded in 1964 by Sargent Shriver, brother-in-law of U.S. President John F. Kennedy, as a last-chance program for low-income young people aged 16 to 24. Now the nation's largest technical training and education program, enrolling 60,000 young men and women in 126 centers across all 50 states, Job Corps participants pay no fees and have the opportunity to earn their high school diplomas.

In 1988, the Department of Labor announced plans to develop a Job Corps Center in a working-class neighborhood in East San Jose. The center design needed to satisfy both the strict parameters of the federal government, which would build the facility, and the interests of the local entities who would operate it. The design also needed to balance the concerns of neighbors worried that a center housing 400 at-risk youth — many of whom had already had a brush with the law — would threaten community safety and well-being. The goal was an efficient, cost-effective campus for educating and supervising this population.

An abandoned, 10-acre elementary school site was identified for redevelopment into a campus that would include dormitories, classrooms, food service, recreational facilities, and healthcare services in both new and rehabilitated structures.

The possibility of working with a population frequently overlooked by society appealed to me both as a designer hungry for more complexity, and as someone raised to pursue social justice. In both instances I saw an opportunity to use architecture to shape a community.

As part of submitting our qualifications, I drove over to the campus. What I encountered shocked me. The passage of time had drained away all color from the empty buildings. The repetitive structures were dated and without character. My first choice would have been to bulldoze the whole thing, but that was not an option.

By way of guidance, the government had distributed a design manual that left little room for creativity. The Department of Labor proposed a cookie-cutter plan that could be applied to all local sites, regardless of region, environment, adjacencies, and other site-specific factors. Within these constraints, it would

LEFT ONE OF THE TYPICAL EXISTING ELEMENTARY SCHOOL BUILDINGS.

RIGHT THE SITE, WITH THE MAIN ENTRY POINT OFF THE *CUL-DE-SAC*, LOWER LEFT.

THE COMPLETED CAMPUS. THE CLOCK TOWER IS AT 9:00 ON THE QUAD; AUTOMOTIVE CLASSES LOWER RIGHT.

be difficult to create something inviting and stimulating.

My sense was that the federal standards were not likely to bring out the best in the San Jose clients the center was to serve. Since many of these young people had dropped out of school at some point, a space that reminded them of elementary school was not likely to inspire them to make a firm commitment and see the program through.

How could we take this black-and-white template and convert it to Technicolor?

I encouraged the local Job Corps representatives to think about the sense of place, the sense of time, and the clientele they sought to assist. How could we create a 24-hour campus uniquely tailored for the young people that they would embrace as their own? How could we foster connections that encouraged participation in sports or extracurricular activities? And, equally important, how could we do this in a way that demonstrated consideration and respect for residential neighbors?

Similar to choreographers of dance and theater, we wanted to arrange the movement of people from one environment to another in order to foster both organized and random interaction. We tried to exploit the potential of sequential spaces to produce dramatic and surprising encounters to encourage positive social interaction and to strike a balance between privacy and participation.

Planners and architects study this relationship between buildings and the spaces they define by using a diagram called a figure-ground.

THE FAÇADE OF THE WOMEN'S DORMITORY; THE TOPS OF THE TRIANGLES ARE CENTRAL SKYLIGHTS.

OVERLEAF THE MEN'S DORMITORY.

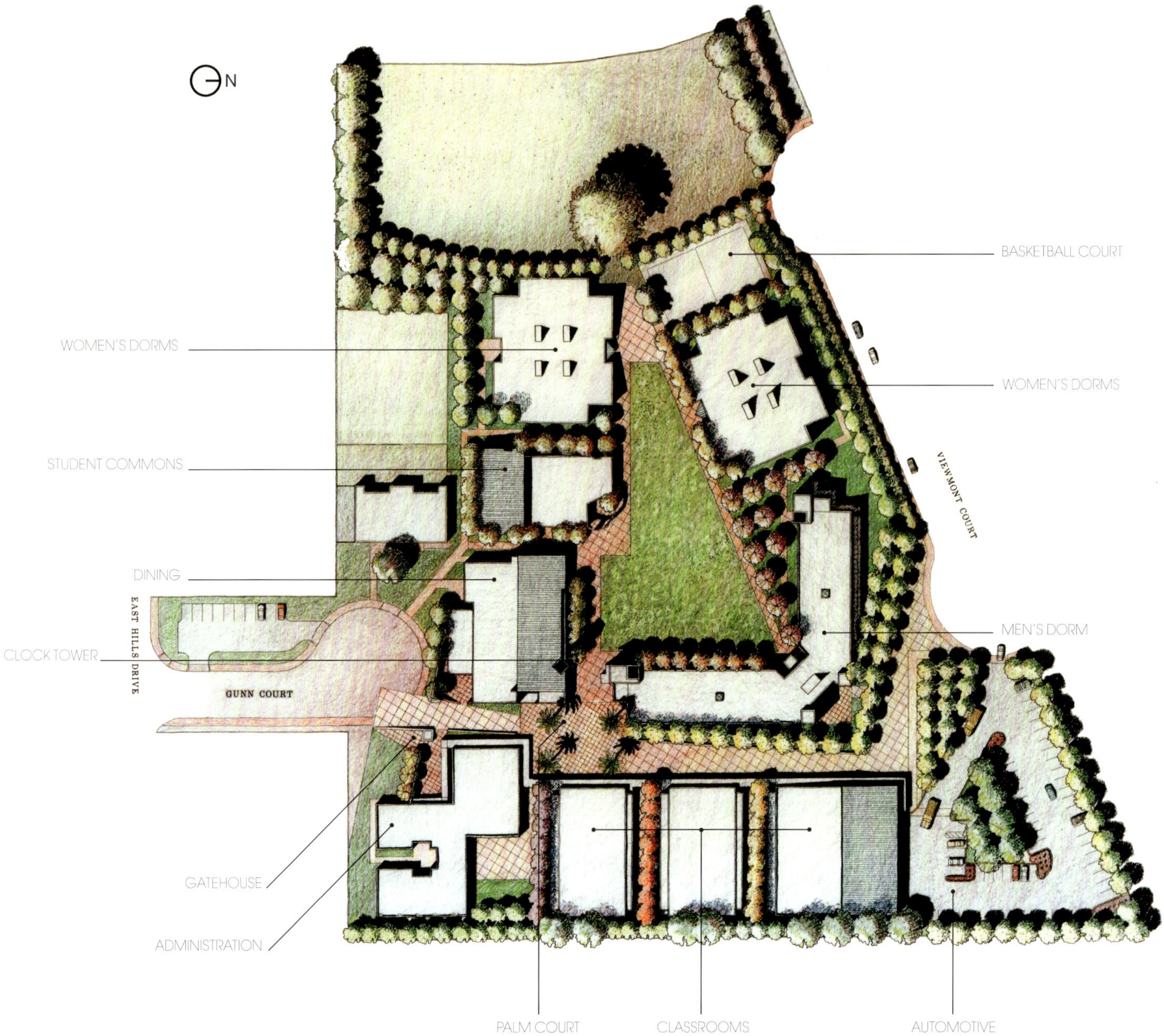
N
BASKETBALL COURT
WOMEN'S DORMS
WOMEN'S DORMS
STUDENT COMMONS
VIEWMONT COURT
DINING
EAST HILLS DRIVE
MEN'S DORM
CLOCK TOWER
GUNN COURT
GATEHOUSE
ADMINISTRATION
PALM COURT
CLASSROOMS
AUTOMOTIVE

Instead of looking at buildings as solid objects, we look at the *spaces* between the buildings, their proportions, and how they connect. For example, in this project we began to see a strong diagonal path that would lead from the entrance to the campus all the way to the education area, crossing the Palm Court on the way and giving shape to the education quad.

The street on which the Job Corps Center is located terminates in a *cul-de-sac* that serves as an entry portal to the community. We planned to utilize landscape paving and sloping entry walls to further guide and funnel visitors to the campus entry. To comply with regulations requiring visitors to sign in and out, a ceremonial guard house would be located at the entry. As with all of the security controls required, we celebrated the spaces, making them more like amusement arcades in color and form, promoting connection between clients and supervisors. The guard house, for example, was whimsical, including an overhang that looked like the tipping of a hat.

Subtly implied in the overall composition was an analogy to the arched entryway of a traditional *hacienda*. We used this analogy to explain our approach to the client: the front door would be the primary entrance, welcoming guests and introducing the aesthetic of the whole.

Balancing traditional forms of the culture in new and hip ways, the entry would deliver visitors to a palm courtyard, where they could choose to go forward to the educational quad, or change course and proceed to the residential areas.

When we shared our conceptual ideas with the interview panel, we were straightforward about our unconventional approach. We had photographed lots of colors, shapes, murals, and patterns from the surrounding neighborhood, and made it clear that we planned to take the same youthful, energetic, and passionate approach in our architecture. Taking aesthetic cues from the Hispanic traditions of the surrounding neighborhood, we proposed an aggressive style, consisting of bold geometric shapes and forms in vibrant shades of purple, yellow, orange, and red that urban youth would find stimulating. Our description of the design opportunity included murals, and even graffiti, to celebrate the culture.

The panel received us enthusiastically, and we were retained as the architect for the project.

But when we returned for the first actual design presentation, our drawings and models, alive with color and geometric forms, drew a gasp from the panel. Despite what we had told them we planned to do, they were not ready for what they saw. We had to backtrack a bit, slowly and methodically explaining our logic to the local Job Corps representatives and the neighbors: we were proposing architecture as a social art, with

OPPOSITE THE PEDESTRIAN ENTRY. A SLOPING WALL GUIDES PEOPLE TO THE HAT-TIP GUARD HOUSE. THE PALM COURT IS IN THE DISTANCE.

ABOVE ANOTHER VIEW OF THE ENTRY.

CLOCKWISE FROM TOP LEFT THE ACADEMIC QUAD. THE GATEWAY LEADS TO THE RESIDENTIAL QUAD. THE PALM COURT IS ON THE LEFT.

THE ARCADE OF THE COMMONS ANIMATES A SHARED SPACE.

THE BASKETBALL COURT IS AN INVITATION TO SOCIALIZE.

OPPOSITE LOOKING BACK TOWARDS THE PALM COURT AND THE ENTRANCE.

EXIT

OPPOSITE, CLOCKWISE FROM TOP

FROM INSIDE THE WOMEN'S DORMITORY, CONNECTIONS ARE BROUGHT TOGETHER FROM OUTSIDE TO IN, AND FROM UPSTAIRS TO THE ENTRY

LARGE WINDOWS BREAK DOWN BARRIERS AND INVITE SOCIAL INTERACTION.

COLORS IN THE DINING AREA BRING THE OUTSIDE IN.

carefully choreographed connections between the campus's various functional areas.

Unfortunately, that was not the end of the process. The Department of Labor still had to approve the design. Our plans apparently generated a lot of discussion in Washington, D.C., but they proved to be too much for the bureaucratic establishment. Our proposal was rejected flat out.

I knew in my bones that our plan was exactly what was needed. Being young and hot-headed, I fought hard to reverse the denial. After several weeks of pushing back, reiterating the wisdom of the approach, and refusing to back down, Washington representatives finally agreed to visit San Jose.

At the face-to-face, we were excited, colorful, passionate, even downright brilliant (at least in our own minds). But once again, our presentation resulted in silence.

"We'll get back to you."

And so we waited, developing alternatives that did not give up on the energy we were determined was necessary for the campus to be able to come alive. Finally, after a month with no clues, we suddenly learned that our design could go ahead. Tempering the good news was the reality that we now faced: it all had to be accomplished within a modest budget. So modest that more than half of the old buildings were to be incorporated into the new design.

To renovate those buildings would require exceedingly thoughtful, yet minimal, interventions that largely depended on daringly deployed new paint. On the bright side, half the building program called for new construction, offering the opportunity to sculpt the space.

We raised and angled parapets to create a fresh geometry for the staid older buildings, and we added geometric appendages to signal hierarchy and wayfinding, such as the entry porch of the recreation building. Our approach accomplished the equivalent of putting a striking accessory on an older item of clothing to update and change its look.

New construction needed to be simple and functional in order to comply with the budget. To give the buildings personality, we found ways to bring natural light into entrances and lobbies. We reserved a portion of the budget to give each building its own unique identity — whether with form, feature, or color.

The Job Corps Center was designed first and foremost with the future clients in mind. The clock tower is the tallest element on the site. A circular arcade portico created a front porch, gathering space, and transition to the recreation building — the most whimsical structure on the campus. The message was clear: "We built this place in celebration of your potential. We're excited about your future, and we want you to launch it from here."

Inside, we reinforced the concept of transforming the required security measures from what could have been oppressive to colorful welcoming points, as we had done with the entrance guard house. We treated control centers as hubs, highlights, and sources of energy. While the entrance and exit of clients and visitors had to be noted, we introduced vertical light monitors to provide natural light in communal areas. Expansive window dimensions reinforced a strong visual connection, allowing residents to see what was happening inside a room before committing to enter, and thus offering a sense of openness and transparency.

Finally the San Jose Job Corps Center was finished, the opening day ribbon cut, faculty hired and students began moving in. We visited from time to time to see whether our navigation clues were working and how the space was bringing strangers together and even helping make friendships. It turned out that the students, if asked, said it was a "happy place." For lives that had often been not so happy, that was a wonderful thing to hear. What we had imagined and hoped for was working.

We were invited to participate in several post-occupancy evaluation discussions with officials from the Department of Labor and local operators. I learned that our concept had shaken many Job Corps officials out of their rigid points of view regarding design. In many cases, federal officials recommended that the architects hired for other Job Corps centers throughout the United States come to see what we had done in San Jose. We were contacted on numerous occasions by other architects from around the country wanting campus tours and copies of our drawings.

As external validation of our work, the AIA awarded the Department of Labor, the San Jose Job Corps Center, and Steinberg Architects a meritorious award for exemplary building projects in Silicon Valley.

More than three decades after it first opened, the San Jose Job Corps Center, still offers some surprises. Most projects that are conceived in vivid colors organized in distinct deployment tend to get blurred or even painted out over time. New paints are purchased that don't quite match the original, and, before long, the basic design essentials are diminished. But not the San Jose Job Corps. The current Director explained: "We have always loved the colors, and have taken great care to make sure they are never altered. It's basic to what this place is."

Maybe more important is an unusual claim for this Job Corps site: it has been so successful in building community that it is the #1 Job Corps center in the country in terms of percentage of current staff and faculty that were once students at the same campus.

A recent graduate remembers the campus as *home* for the years she was there. And, even more importantly, she got her first exposure to criminal justice, in a positive way, when she was given responsibility to work the dormitory's red and purple control center. Now, she's training at the Sacramento Police Academy, on her way to becoming a professional law enforcement officer.

ABOVE THE RED COLUMNS SAY "WELCOME TO THE HEART OF YOUR COMMUNITY."

OPPOSITE THE REQUIRED CONTROL CENTER IS TRANSFORMED INTO A POINT OF WELCOME.

4 ARCHITECTURE EXISTS IN TENSION WITH NATURE

ARCHITECTURE
STRIVES TO CO-EXIST
WITH NATURE'S FORCES
INCLUDING GRAVITY,
WATER, AND LIGHT.

DAVIS HIGH SCHOOL LIBRARY COMPLEX

Location	Davis, California
Latitude/Longitude	38°33'21.1"N 121°45'03.1"W
Client	Davis Unified School District
Date	1992–99
Size	33,000 sq ft
Awards	American Institute of Architects, Award of Merit, 1999
	American Institute of Architects, Leroy Greene Award, 1999

RAIN, STONES, PEBBLES, BAMBOO

When I was a young architect, I didn't fully understand the opportunity that forces such as gravity, energy, water, and the sun presented to a designer. Lacking that understanding, I either downplayed or tried to bend the forces of nature to fit my vision: steel and concrete, arches and trusses could battle gravity; slate, tar, and endless caulking could hold back moisture; shades, awnings, and slats could filter light.

But a lesson learned when our firm expanded to China refined my thinking. During an extended battle with a number of human forces that were undermining the quality of a project I was passionate about, my partner Henry Zeng took me to the World Heritage site of Dujiangyan west of Chengdu, which celebrates both the mythology and the reality of attempts to control the Minjiang River. There, Henry told me a story about rain, stones, pebbles, and bamboo.

Until the 3rd century BCE, the Chengdu plain was frequently plagued by floods. Every year when the rains came, the water collected in the mountains and eventually flooded one of the most fertile valleys in Western China, often wiping out the season's crops.

The legendary ruler Gun the Great was tasked with devising a system to control the flooding. He spent more than nine years building a series of massive dikes and enormous dams in an effort to control the floodwaters. The work required the labor of thousands of men who moved millions of tons of rock. And yet, no matter how high the dams were built, year after year, when the rainy seasons came, the waters spilled over the dams, filling the valley with silt and destroying the crops.

Gun's son, Yu, assumed his father's lifework to beat back the annual deluge. However, instead of erecting barriers to control the floodwaters, he took his time to make a careful and meticulous study of the river's flow.

His observations led Yu to conceive an approach more oriented toward harnessing and channeling the river's energy than containing and controlling it. To divide and slow the river, he created an artificial island, with the end of the island that faced the current shaped like a fish's mouth.

Eventually, part of the river was shunted to a vast collection area. Yu devised an artificial levee constructed from long, sausage-shaped baskets of woven bamboo filled with stones and held in place by wooden tripods, which directed the runoff from the fields out to the sea, substantially reducing the water levels so that the land could be reliably cultivated. In time, the region around the Chengdu plain, Sichuan Province, became known as the Heavenly State. And over two thousand years later, Yu remains a renowned figure in Chinese history.

The experience changed the way I thought about my conflicts of the moment, and eventually changed the way I thought about the inherent tension between nature and the built environment. Standing on the bridge that overlooks the fish's head, which is still there and still slowing the river, I began to change the way I engaged with life.

The business of running an architecture firm entails episodic growth and change punctuated by adjustment to external influences — not only natural conditions, but political, and economic trends as well. Key among those external factors is the inevitable ebb and flow of the economy. In the span of just ten years, our firm suffered through three recessions. Recessions in 1980 and 1982 were induced by the Federal Reserve Board raising interest rates to help combat inflation; the 1989 recession emerged from the savings and loan crisis and lasted nine long months. There were countless nights during each bleak period that I awoke in a cold sweat, panicking over payroll and agonizing over who would stay and who I would have to let go. Emerging from the worst of times, I was determined to find a way to mitigate these extreme swings.

During a recession, when the private sector is in decline, government-funded projects are among the few sources of architectural work. They are demanding to win, but offer a valuable lifeline in uncertain economic times.

Smarting from the setback of so many recessions, and eager to capitalize on the explosion in school facility renovation and construction, our firm pursued district architect positions aggressively, including in the town of Davis, California, just west of Sacramento.

With a population of 65,000, the city of Davis, California, was initially a farming community. The complexion shifted in 1959, when the Regents of the University of California opened a new campus in Davis, transforming it into a college town.

Davis combines the advantages of a family-friendly small town with the numerous intellectual, recreational, and cultural activities the campus offers. Its well-educated residents pay a premium to live there, and have high expectations for public services, including the education of their children. And everything that is developed must be done with sustainability at its heart.

You can imagine my elation when I was selected as the District Architect for Davis, which led to my spending a day or two there every week over a period of several years, assessing existing buildings and their conditions, gathering input from a broad range of stakeholders, and developing a vision with district staff and consultants.

The payoff for all of this legwork was a design plum: the opportunity to develop a centerpiece for Davis High School: the new library complex.

I met with the full range of interested parties, from students to the local Rotary Club, to glean their thoughts on a number of school-related issues, especially focusing on the high school library. The students challenged us to create a library that would serve as an aspirational space, reflecting their optimism while updating the image of the school. They wanted a building with "attitude," a gathering place that reflected both their quest for knowledge and their commitment to environmental responsibility.

As District Architect, it was my job to roll up all the facility assessments, focus groups, and community input to not only create but also to help "sell" the master plan to the voters.

The day of the election I drove up to Davis, eager to be among the team members who had worked so hard to bring our education facilities master plan to the finish line. We gathered,

THE NEW LIBRARY COMPLEX (RED) WITHIN THE EXISTING CAMPUS SETTING (PURPLE).

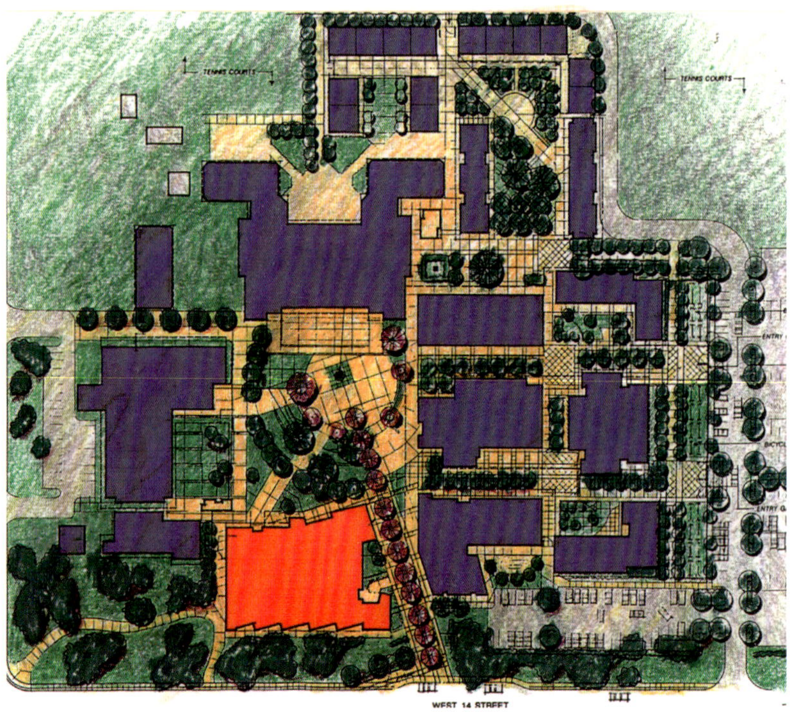

FIRST-FLOOR PLAN OF THE DAVIS HIGH SCHOOL LIBRARY COMPLEX.

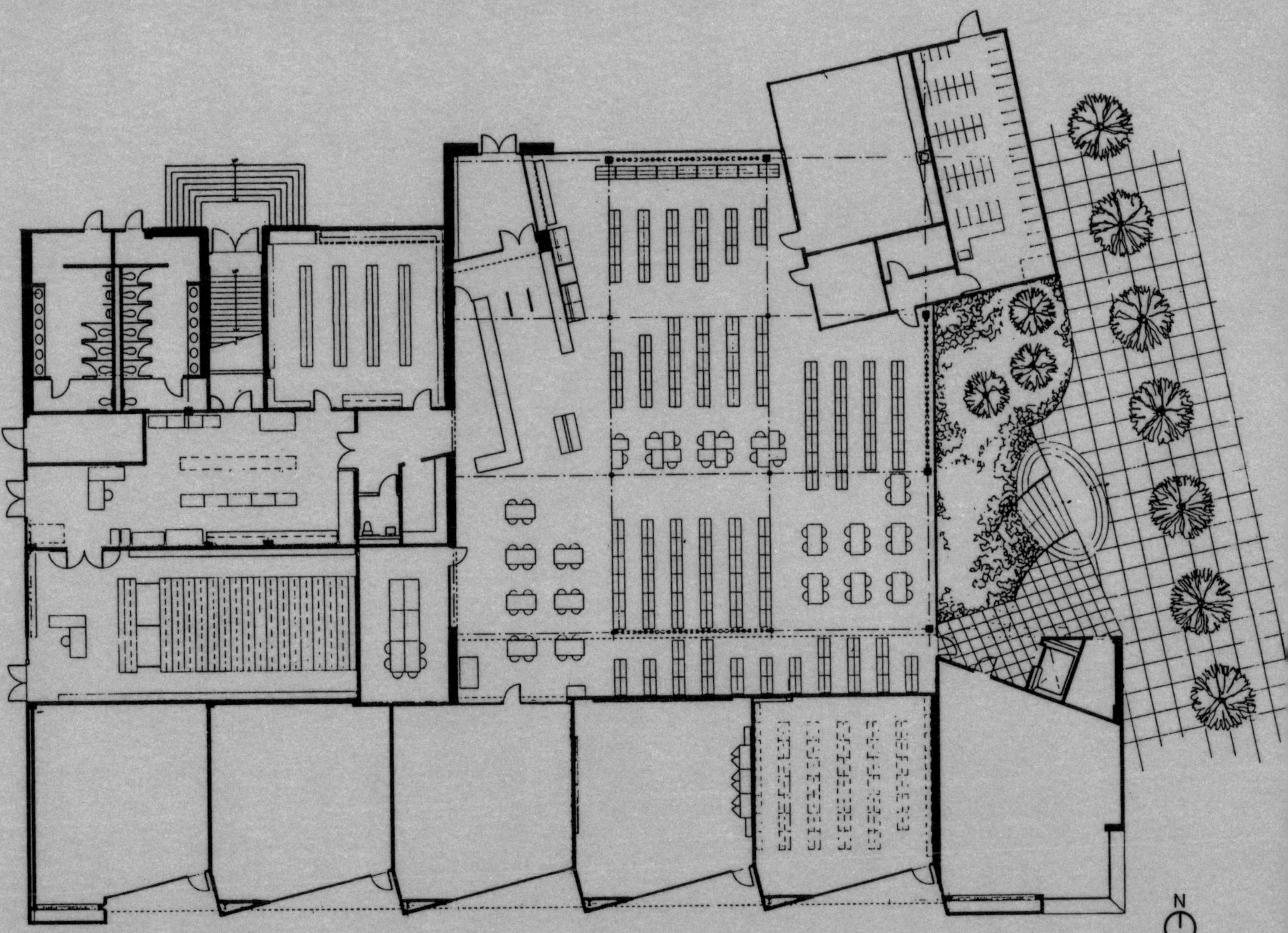

awaiting election returns, eating pizza straight out of delivery boxes, and nervously making small talk until the wee hours of the morning, when, at last, we got the verdict: Davis residents had approved the parcel tax to fund school facility improvements by a whopping seventy percent. Champagne corks popped! Cake was served!

LIGHT

The first question I ask when visiting a site is, "Where is North?" While on the site I want to set my compass so that I can begin tracking the movement of the sun across the hours in the day and the seasons of the year. As we walked the high school campus with the district's leadership, I took note that the long sides of the proposed building site's rectangular shape were oriented north-south — the optimal position to take advantage of indirect northern light while offering options to control the harsh light from the south. Our group's conversation quickly turned to the physical and spiritual characteristics of light.

A lifetime observing my father's masterful use of light as reinforcement for emotional well-being provided a context for the site analysis. Plus, I couldn't help but think of abundant idioms: when you "see the light," or "shed light" on a subject, you are gaining intellectual insight. "Light at the end of the tunnel" indicates a hopeful outcome. When you "bring information to light" you are surfacing a new idea. All of these related to the acquisition of the knowledge that is metaphorically and literally housed in a library. I began to imagine a dialogue between nature and a building that would address not only the functional but also the emotional and aspirational expectations of the students.

THE INTERPLAY BETWEEN THE COMPONENTS THAT COMPRISE THE COMPLEX: NINE CLASSROOMS (YELLOW) LINE TWO SIDES OF THE LIBRARY (BLUE) WHILE THE MULTIPURPOSE ROOM (RED) CARVES INTO A CORNER ON THE OPPOSITE SIDE.

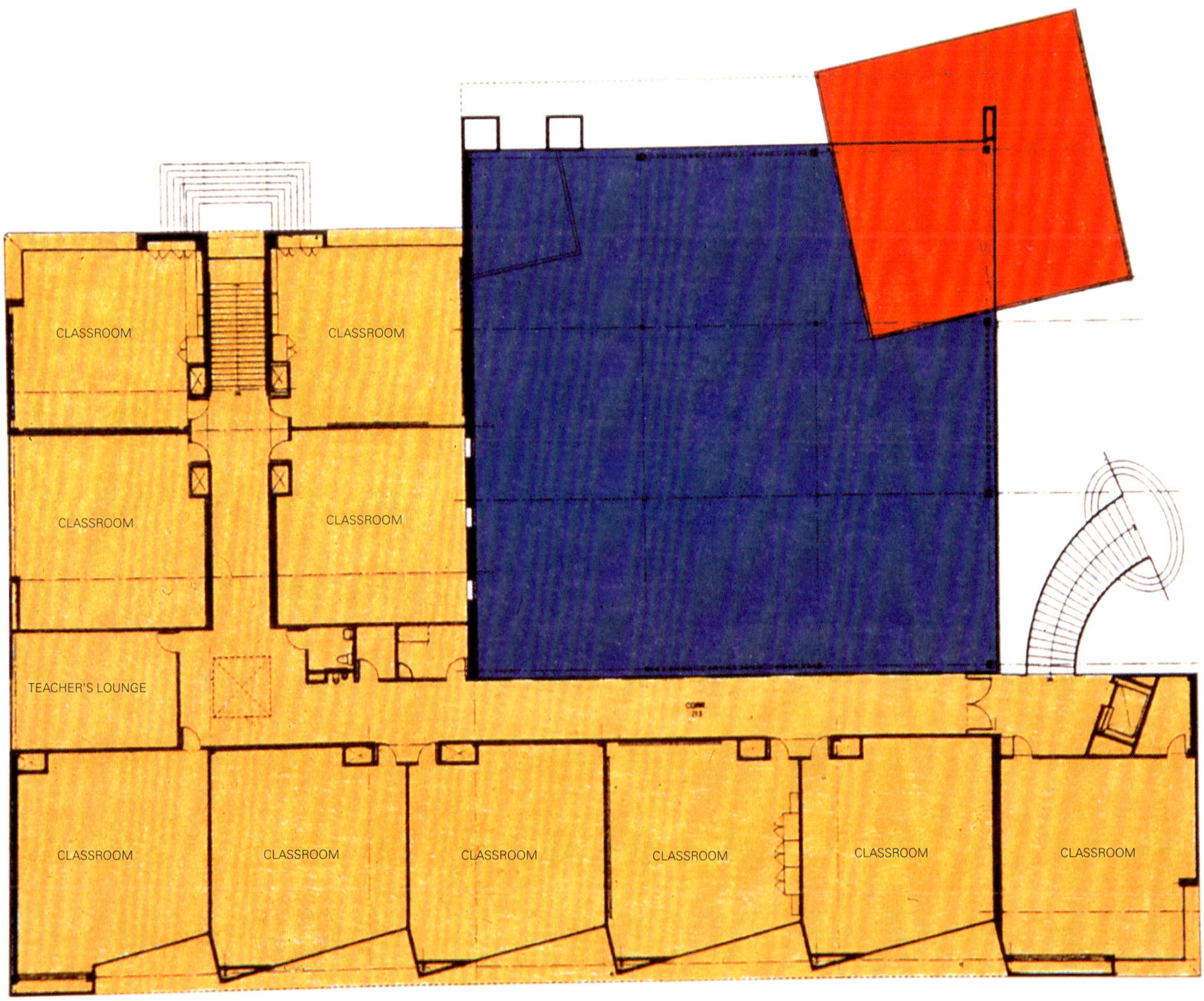

The site analysis, combined with two years of immersion in the community, led to our big idea: we would celebrate the properties of natural light, optimizing inspiration and energy efficiency.

I added a project goal of my own: that the building would serve as a teaching tool about architecture itself. By making the function of the building's components obvious, the students would be able to see that they were occupying a structure in which every supporting element was contributing to the efficiency of the building.

The library complex entailed three components: a new library, an addition of nine classrooms, and a multipurpose room that would serve both the school and the community, functioning as a teaching space during school hours, and as a community space after school.

From the quad, the expansive new library was primary; the classroom addition and meeting room would play supporting roles. The classroom component was set back further from the quad than the library, underscoring its secondary role, while the canted meeting room bit into the library's corner.

USING THE SAME COLOR-CODING SYSTEM AS P91, THE SKETCH SHOWS THE VIEW OF THE COMPLEX FROM THE QUAD, INCLUDING THE NORTH-FACING WINDOW WALL.

Although the meeting room was the smallest component of the composition, by pivoting its orientation to interrupt the rectangle of the quad, we asserted its strategic importance as a resource for both the school and the community, and as a kind of 'gate keeper' on the quad.

WATER

My professors at Cal repeatedly emphasized the importance of drawing a building in section — that is, slicing through a building to help analyze spatial relationships between inside and outside and the characteristics of the volumes enclosed.

Our first attempts at the section drawing explored both sloped as well as flat-roof options, both of which seemed pedestrian. We began to test alternatives, and soon we found the right spirit in an *inverted bow* roof. Bow roofs are rare. For starters, the inverted bow suffers from the appearance that it will collect rather than shed rainwater, which easily leads to the cardinal sin of architecture: water leaking into a building. However, as we worked through the pros and cons of various roof designs, responding to and pushing back against nature's forces grew more and more compelling to me. In contrast to the more common flat- or gabled-roof shapes, the counterpoint of both welcoming and resisting nature's forces and the tension it created gave a playful profile to the building. The water issue? We created a hidden 'cricket' to raise and angle the center of the bottom of the bow, which ultimately directed the water to perimeter downspouts. Problem solved.

Most importantly, the roof style and shape was ideal for capturing and balancing daylight. A two-story, north-facing window wall faced the quad and captured the maximum amount of northern indirect natural light without the heat gain and the corresponding need to cool the space. An added benefit was the connection between the library and the quad, allowing the visual energy of one to feed the other.

As the roofline's bow curved upward to the south, nestled between the lower classrooms and an extended roof overhang, we inserted a clerestory window the full length of the library that allowed shaded south light to wash the ceiling and balance the light levels throughout the space.

Bow-shaped windows on the east façade, echoing the geometry of the roof, washed the gentle curve of the ceiling and the horizontal floor plane with natural light and intentionally directed views up to the sky or down to the adjacent garden. This had the effect of further balancing the north and south light in the room, physically warming the space by capturing the early morning sunshine and focusing students' sightlines on the earth and sky — the very forces of nature with which the library strove to harmonize. We tempered the harsh afternoon light — the most difficult to control — by nestling the south and west façades of the library into the crook of the L-shaped classroom building.

We had gone to great lengths to capture indirect, natural light, so the last thing we wanted was to introduce glare from artificial lighting that would reflect on computer screens. Capitalizing on our investment in creating a gracefully sloping roof, we chose to light the library with high-efficiency, indirect light that would bounce off and give prominence to the ceiling.

SCALE

Larger volumes can be appropriate for public buildings that accommodate many people, but we also needed to ensure that individuals and

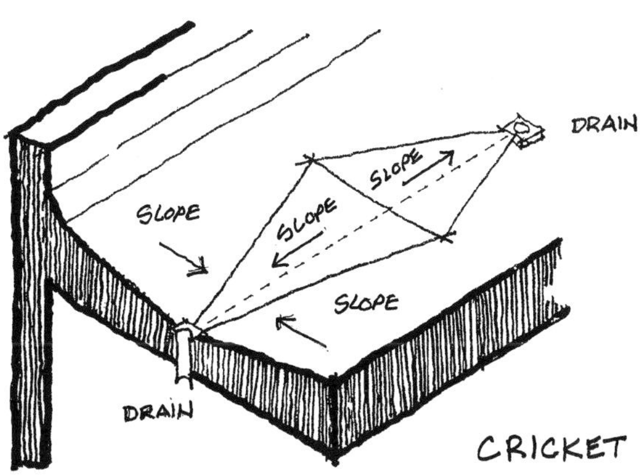

SECTION OF THE LIBRARY. THE FLOOR-TO-CEILING WINDOWS ON THE RIGHT FACE NORTH; THE LARGE OVERHANG ON THE LEFT SHADES THE SOUTH-FACING GLASS. THE ENTRY AIR-LOCK (REAR RIGHT) BUFFERS THE INTERIOR FROM PREVAILING

WINDS. THE RED STEEL-BRACE FRAME AND INTEGRATED BOUNCE LIGHTING, WITH YELLOW HVAC DUCTS, REVEAL HOW THE BUILDING OPERATES. ON THE LEFT AND REAR WALLS, WINDOWS LOOK INTO THE LIBRARY FROM THE CLASSROOMS.

small groups were not overwhelmed. In addition to warping upward on the perimeter — ideal for capturing maximum natural light — the bowed roof drooped to its lowest point in the center of the library, mitigating the monumentality of the volume to some extent, though not completely. In an effort to further make the space feel more intimate, we made two smaller-scale interventions. The first was the angled meeting room that notched into the library volume; the second was a windowed, geometric double-door airlock required to prevent wind from blowing into the building. Both provided single-story references that kept the space closely related to a more human scale.

TECTONICS

Addressing the obligatory gravity and seismic requirements of the building code, we consciously emphasized the structural steel-braced frame, including the triangulated diagonals that illustrated how the building would resist lateral movement in the event of an earthquake. And in case they didn't catch the students' attention, we painted them red!

THERMAL

In the same spirit of revealing how the building functioned, we highlighted heating, ventilation, air conditioning, and electrical systems. A secondary benefit of exposing these as visual elements was the introduction of scale and visual interest to the interior character of the space. Aluminum air ducts were mounted on the steel structure at a mid-height between the floor and ceiling, reducing the perceived height of the space. This also added efficiency to operational costs: hot air, which rises, traditionally blown downward by vents at the ceiling level, was now

THE LOWER WINDOWS ON THE EAST WALL (REAR) OFFER THE SEATED STUDENT A VIEW OF THE GARDEN. THE WALL'S UPPER WINDOWS FLOAT THE ROOF AND WARM THE INTERIOR WITH THE MORNING SUN.

being distributed with less distance to travel to reach the people at floor level.

PLANETARY MOTION

Our studies tracking the sun's impact on the southern side of the classroom building during various seasons and times of day yielded a complex challenge. We wanted to maximize indirect light into the classrooms, while minimizing heat gain. We crafted a solution with carefully calibrated overhangs, perimeter walls beveled to achieve a slightly more southeasterly direction, and by varying window height calibrated to match the sun's movement. Horizontal, reflective light shelves mounted at door height bounced indirect light deeper into the interior spaces, further reducing the need for artificial lighting and corresponding cooling.

These complex classroom windows gave the street-facing side of the classroom building a distinctive character, making it clear that intention was taken to make these spaces energy efficient as well as delightful to the students working inside. The terraces providing access to first-floor classrooms offered a welcoming place for people to linger, bringing life to the public-facing side of the campus and integrating it with the Davis community.

Some of the classrooms' windows gave direct views into the library; other classrooms with their pivoted walls created a different benefit. In a typical rectangular classroom, students face the teacher in rigid geometry. Here, the beveled walls had the effect of shifting the teacher's desk from the front of the room to the corner, while the descending height of the windowsill focused natural light toward the teaching walls to the left and right of the instructor. The less rigid seating arrangement imposed by these factors, combined with the use of two teaching walls, offered more teaching flexibility and a more free-form, relaxed atmosphere.

UNITY

The Davis High School Library Complex tells a story of balancing the forces of nature with a person-made environment. We created a dynamic space where young people could immerse themselves in a repository of knowledge, naturally illuminated, and integrated with the city. The complex also serves as a more general teaching tool that tells how buildings can comfortably exist in tension with nature.

As I learned from Gun the younger, the forces of Mother Nature are powerful. We do not need to confront them. Instead, we should engage with them.

Shall we dance?

BELOW LEFT THE AIR-LOCK CREATES A SHARP TRANSITION FROM QUAD ACTIVITIES TO THE INTERIOR STUDY. GLASS SHELVING PROVIDES DISPLAY SPACE.

BELOW RIGHT ANGLED WINDOWS CANT THE INTERIOR, PLACING THE TEACHER BETWEEN TWO TEACHING WALLS AND CREATING A MORE RELAXED ATMOSPHERE.

RIGHT THE BUILDING PROVIDES A NEW AND DYNAMIC ENTRY TO THE CAMPUS.

BELOW SOUTH-FACING WINDOWS TRACK THE SUN, MAXIMIZING INDIRECT LIGHT, SUPPLEMENTED BY THE HORIZONTAL LIGHT SHELVES THAT BOUNCE DEEP INTO THE CLASSROOMS. THE WIDE TERRACE INVITES STUDENTS TO CONGREGATE, BREAKING DOWN THE BOUNDARIES ON THE COMMUNITY-FACING SIDE OF THE COMPLEX.

THE GARDEN VISIBLE FROM THE EASTERN SIDE OF THE LIBRARY. THE INTERSECTION BETWEEN THE MEETING ROOM ON THE RIGHT AND THE LIBRARY IS EXAGGERATED BY THE GLASS SEAM.

THE FLAT, RECTANGULAR, MEETING-ROOM WALL SETS A DEAD-NEUTRAL STAGE AS A TRANSITION INTO THE QUAD.

5
Architecture is Storytelling

At its best, architecture originates from a single organizing narrative, and every supporting element is an expression of that same force.

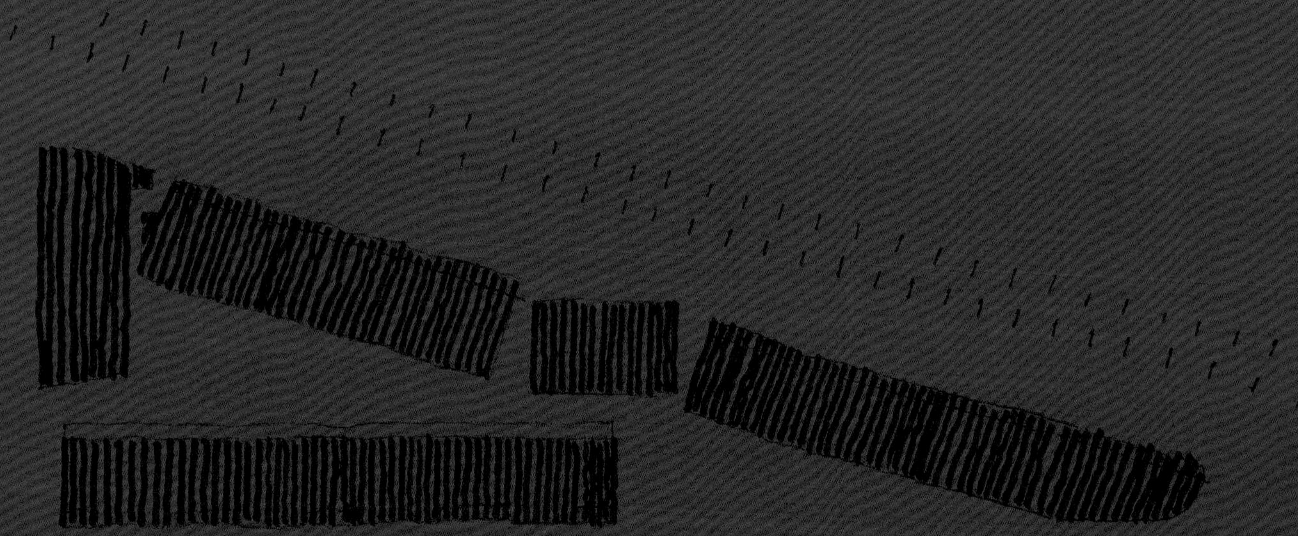

MARKETHOUSE LOFTS

Location	San Jose, California
Latitude/Longitude	37°21'16.2"N 121°53'38.4"W
Client	Sares Regis
Date	2000–05
Size	65,400 sq ft

THE TRAIN WRECK

Back in the days before email and shared, cloud-based drives, we typically sent our evolving design plans to our clients via fax. In this particular project, I was trying to get the right feel for the five buildings I was designing, putting them askew here and there.

My client received the plans on his state-of-the-art, sheet-fed fax machine and did his best to cut, fold, and tape together the different configurations in the correct sequences. But the triangular geometry of the site and the various grids bordering it complicated the task, and the client never knew for sure if he was placing the pages properly. One day he called me, utterly frustrated and completely unable to make sense of the latest fax transmission.

"This is a train wreck!" he lamented.

The story for Markethouse Lofts was born.

My approach to architecture as storytelling is a natural outgrowth of my documentary filmmaking career, as well as the influence of my father, a wonderful storyteller.

The process of creating a documentary film begins with the filmmaker amassing a wide variety of material, with no sure sense of how it ultimately will be used. The footage is simply raw material for the eventual editorial process. Initially, there is no beginning, middle, or end — the essentials of a good story.

Through my academic work at New York University's Tisch School of the Arts, followed by several large-form, documentary film projects, the process of first capturing a huge range of material and eventually transforming it into a coherent and meaningful narrative became a deeply ingrained part of me.

As I developed as an architect, storytelling became an integral aspect of my practice. Narrative offers the architect a chance to deepen a user's emotional connection to place. Without that clearly articulated tie to place, architecture is far less likely to resonate. If context is absent, people are still able to admire a building's beauty, but knowing the story the structure is telling creates a much richer appreciation.

Sergei Eisenstein, one of the most important pioneers of early cinema, was trained as an architect. He is credited with developing a film technique known as montage, in which a series of shots are edited into a sequence intended to stimulate emotion.

The best-known example of Eisenstein's technique occurs in his 1925 silent propaganda film, *Battleship Potemkin*. In rapid cuts depicting the retribution of the Cossack soldiers on the Odessa Steps, the viewer sees soldiers marching in single file, revealing a dead body as they march over it (*cut*) a mother, with a baby carriage at the top of a long, stone staircase, hesitates (*cut*) the soldiers shoot (*cut*) the mother is shot (*cut*) the carriage carrying an infant teeters, threatening to break loose from the guiding hand of the (*cut*) baby's mother, and then (*cut*) it careens uncontrollably down the steep and sweeping staircase with (*cut*) (*cut*) (*cut*) the mother slowly dropping as the carriage descends stair after stair and then (*cut*) the cannon turret of the Battleship Potemkin.

A child in danger always elicits an emotional response, and none more so than a baby in a buggy tumbling down corpse-littered steps. The pram element is specifically designed to manipulate the emotions, to make the viewer sympathize with the downtrodden masses against the machine-like, murdering force of the Cossacks.

Architecture can also stimulate an emotional response. Frank Lloyd Wright was a master at designing series of environmental experiences to evoke an affecting reaction. You might enter a Wright building through a low, dark vestibule that opens onto a grand, high-ceilinged space. The visitor feels at first very cramped and needing to bow their head before emerging into a soaring, light-filled volume. Wright's dynamic contrast evokes an intense human response.

Urban planners call this progression of experiences *serial visioning*. The progress of travel is illuminated by a series of contrasts that affect perception, resulting in an emotional journey for the person coming through a new space for the first time, and possibly each time they move through the space.

A small book that dramatically discusses serial visioning has had a powerful impact on me. *The Concise Townscape* (Architectural Press, 1961) by Gordon Cullen describes moving through an urban expanse, weaving elements together to reveal the drama of the city. On page 10, Cullen writes:

> Suppose you are visiting one of the hill towns in the south of France. You climb laboriously up the winding road and eventually find yourself in a tiny village street at the summit. You feel thirsty and go to a nearby restaurant, your drink is served to you on a veranda, and as you go out to it you find to your exhilaration or horror that the veranda is cantilevered out over a thousand-foot drop. By this device of the containment (street) and the revelation (cantilever) the fact of height is dramatized and made real.

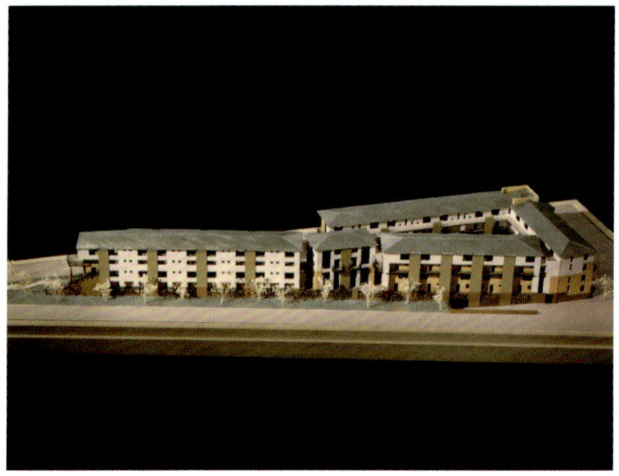

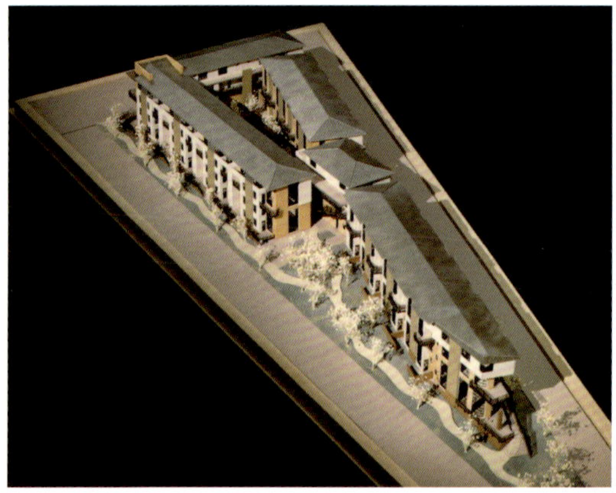

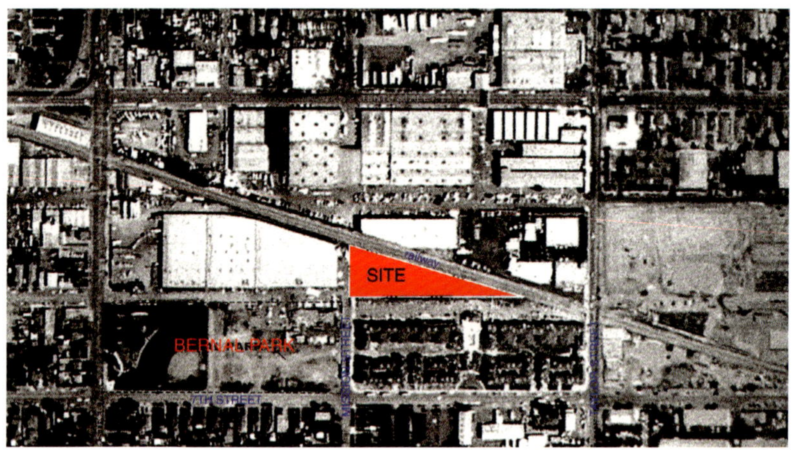

FROM TOP

MODEL VIEW ACROSS THE RAILROAD TRACKS. EACH OF THE FIVE BUILDINGS REFLECTS A DIFFERENT TYPE OF BOXCAR, STREWN AROUND AFTER THE WRECK.

THE CRASH APPEARS TO HAVE FORMED TWO COURTYARDS.

BEFORE THE DISASTER, A USELESS FRAGMENT OF LAND.

In encountering such a progression, even those who don't know what serial visioning is, experience a powerful force. And, once they have experienced the story, they can't ever see things the same way again.

Our commission to design high-density housing in an older, industrial neighborhood was part of a broader redevelopment effort known as the Jackson-Taylor Specific Plan. The larger plan's 80-acre parcel aimed to create a residential, retail, and industrial community. The surrounding area was anchored by Bini's Bar and Grill, an old-world restaurant where lawyers bellied up to the massive, dark-stained wood bar alongside off-duty police officers, painters, and cowboys. It was a real melting pot, and we wanted to maintain that spirit as we thought through the residential project and who ultimately would inhabit it.

TRACKS ON THE LEFT, AN EXISTING APARTMENT BUILDING ON THE RIGHT — THE WRECK HAD NOWHERE TO GO.

Our site was an acute-triangle, 1.5-acre parcel hard up against Union Pacific railroad tracks on one long side. A large apartment complex and the loading doors of a warehouse pinched the site off from the street and from a park not far away.

In a nod to the district's history of canneries, flower marts, and a farmers market, we planned to model Markethouse on the repurposing of industrial buildings into residential lofts on the United States' East Coast. We hoped to attract urban pioneers to a new type of housing: the industrial loft that at the time represented something new in San Jose.

A triangular site is inherently inefficient. The fact of two acute angles compounds the architect's challenge. The site's narrow dimensions, combined with the need to buffer the noise and vibrations from passing freight trains, dictated the slim width of our buildings. In a departure from the more standard apartment buildings with units on both sides of a center corridor, our living spaces lined only one side of long hallways — the side farthest from the tracks.

We choose to create five buildings of varying lengths, with a total of 53 double-height, residential lofts, stacked two high, each offering

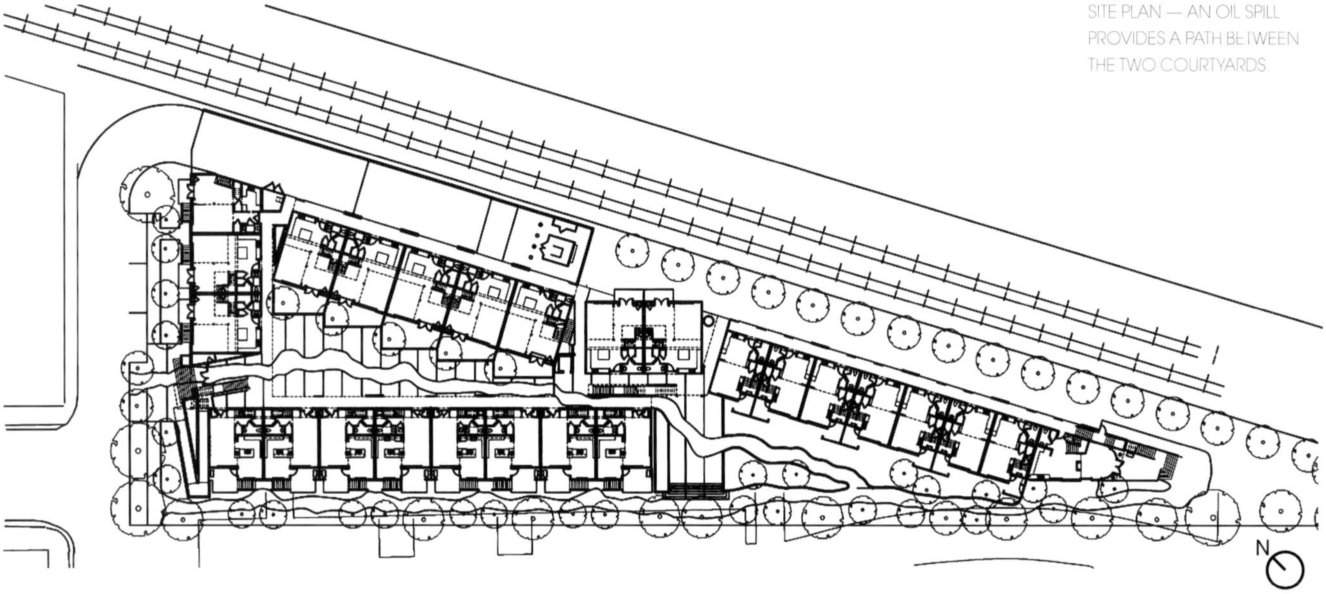

SITE PLAN — AN OIL SPILL PROVIDES A PATH BETWEEN THE TWO COURTYARDS

a different floorplan. In two of the buildings the apartments faced outward to the public streets, and two buildings faced the interior of the complex. A fifth, four-unit building faced the tracks. In four of the five buildings, the hallways buffered the sound from the tracks.

One building evoked the elongated, linear shape of a train, including the aerodynamic, curved, leading edge of a locomotive. Tapered metal siding down the length of the exterior wall and double-height glass were reminiscent of the front view of a train. A private, steep stairway up to a landing resembled the engineer's platform. Metal railings felt like the cowcatcher on the front of a locomotive, placed to remove debris encountered on the tracks.

We designed a second building to evoke a caboose. Its adjacent, accessibility ramp looked like it could be used to wheel freight on board. An angled exit stair celebrated the rear of the caboose that freeloaders could grab as the train sped by. Metal roofing peeled down the siding to enclose a modern-day overlook suitable for a political candidate's whistle-stop tour.

Industrial windows and standing-seam metal roofs folded partially down the vertical face of the boxcars, framing a rhythmic pattern including subtle façade variations of deep recesses overlaid with repeating red panels. Taken together, the panels conjured telegraph poles zipping by as a passenger might witness looking out of the train window. In strategic locations, the exteriors were peeled away as if the boxcars had derailed and slid along the ground, exposing mangled layers of metal balconies, bay windows, stairs, railings, and canopies.

We designed the walking path through the complex, providing access to most of the units,

WHAT REMAINS OF THE ENGINE, WITH THE ENGINEER'S PLATFORM ABOVE, AND BELOW THAT, THE ROUNDED FRONT OF THE COWCATCHER.

'he phrase **make the grade**, or succeed at something, might come from the idea of railroads going up a gradient or incline.

LEFT GAPING HOLES IN THE TWISTED METAL PROVIDE SHADE.

BELOW THE RED VERTICALS SUGGEST A MEMORY OF TELEGRAPH POLES FLASHING BY. ON THE GROUND, A WAVE RETRACES THE OIL SPILL.

You might not be surprised that this term for getting distracted or off topic comes from an actual **sidetrack**

— a secondary track or line for a train. The literal meaning dates from c.1828, while *the figurative use starts about 30 years later.*

OPPOSITE THE CABOOSE PROVIDES A PLATFORM FOR A WHISTLE-STOP TOUR. HANDRAILS OFFER FREELOADERS EASY ON AND OFF.

2
1

DECK/
PATOP
LIVE
ZONE
Live
up
COAT
LAUNDRY
FAT
ZONE
Eat
W/C
FIRST LEVEL
OPEN
TO
BELOW
up
Sleep
CLOSET
SLEEP
ZONE
BATH
SECOND LEVEL

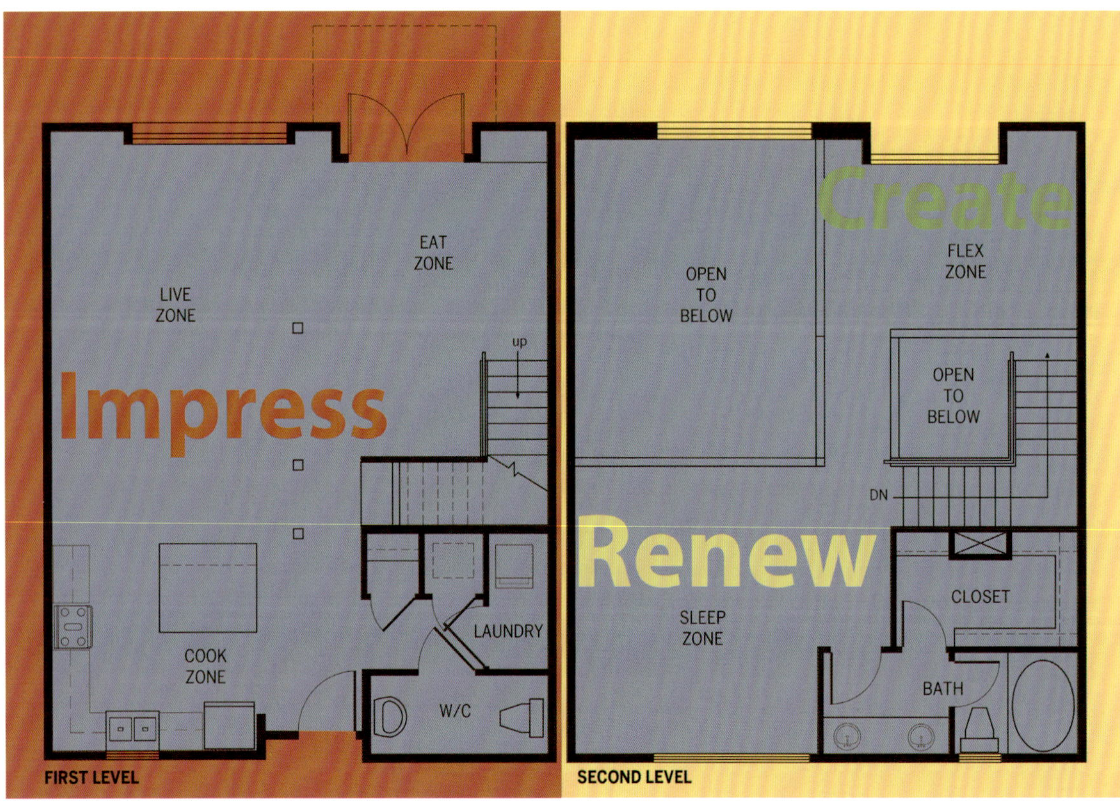
EAT
ZONE
LIVE
ZONE
up
Impress
COOK
ZONE
LAUNDRY
W/C
FIRST LEVEL
Create
OPEN
TO
BELOW
FLEX
ZONE
OPEN
TO
BELOW
DN
Renew
SLEEP
ZONE
CLOSET
BATH
SECOND LEVEL

OPPOSITE THE BROCHURE CONVEYS THE GLORIES OF OLD TERMINAL ANNOUNCEMENT BOARDS, WITH THEIR EVER-CLACKING SPLIT-FLAP DISPLAYS.

RIGHT STEEP STAIRS FEEL AS IF THEY LEAD TO AN UPPER BERTH IN A PULLMAN SLEEPER, WHILE THE HIGH WINDOWS WHISPER "VISTA DOME."

BELOW THE LOFT IS ACCESSED VIA A NARROW, CABLED BRIDGE.

to look like an oil spill streaming across the site of an accident. The randomly configured stone path graphically connects the pedestrian circulation through the pinch point that defines the two courtyards — one enclosed and one partially open. Oversized, rounded royal blue accent flower pots suggested the wheels.

Similar to the compact utilization and efficiencies of space on a train, no space was wasted inside the units. Multiple functions — socializing, working, eating, and sleeping — were placed within a single space, organized through the use of varied-height spaces, stairs and columns.

The double-height windows conveyed the special feeling of taking a vacation, traveling to a unique destination and looking out of a train window. In a romantic evocation of rail travel, sleeping lofts accessed by stairs mimicked the fold-down berths in a train's sleeper car.

Even the project's marketing materials expressed the train imagery. We designed the contemporary townhomes to appeal to urban pioneers seeking an alternative to traditional, suburban housing options. Aiming to attract hip city dwellers who, more than likely, commuted by train, the graphic format referenced the split-flap clacking displays prevalent in railroad stations. We chose attention-grabbing colors to catch the eye of rushing commuters: purple, yellow-green, terracotta, and blue-gray.

Because the area was devoid of the ordinary components of a residential neighborhood, the lofts ultimately became a self-contained community. Responding to conditions that appeared to be less than ideal and looking for the magic in the unique characteristics of the site, we were able to reframe the lack of context, the parcel shape, the railroad tracks, and the noise from negative elements as a positive, community-building catalyst for future development. Inspired by the image of a "train wreck," the space we

sculpted not only helped shape the lives of the residents of Markethouse Lofts but also set a standard for design quality that initiated a trajectory for this balance of the district to become one of downtown's most livable and enduring neighborhoods.

Does everyone who lives or visits the lofts know that they are visiting a train wreck? It doesn't really make any difference. They will sense that something is going on, something zany that's holding the place together, making it feel unique and delightful. A place where you might want to linger for a while with a child and tell a story.

"Once upon a time there was a little train…"

BELOW THE AERODYNAMIC ENGINE AND THE ENGINEER'S STEEP ACCESS STAIRS.

OPPOSITE THE WRECK AND THE TRACKS IN HARMONY.

While most of us know a **turntable** as another word for a record player, it originated as a railroad term referring to a revolving platform that was used for turning trains.

6 ARCHITECTURE TELLS US HOW TO USE IT

A building's function, hierarchy, and navigation should support an intuitive understanding.

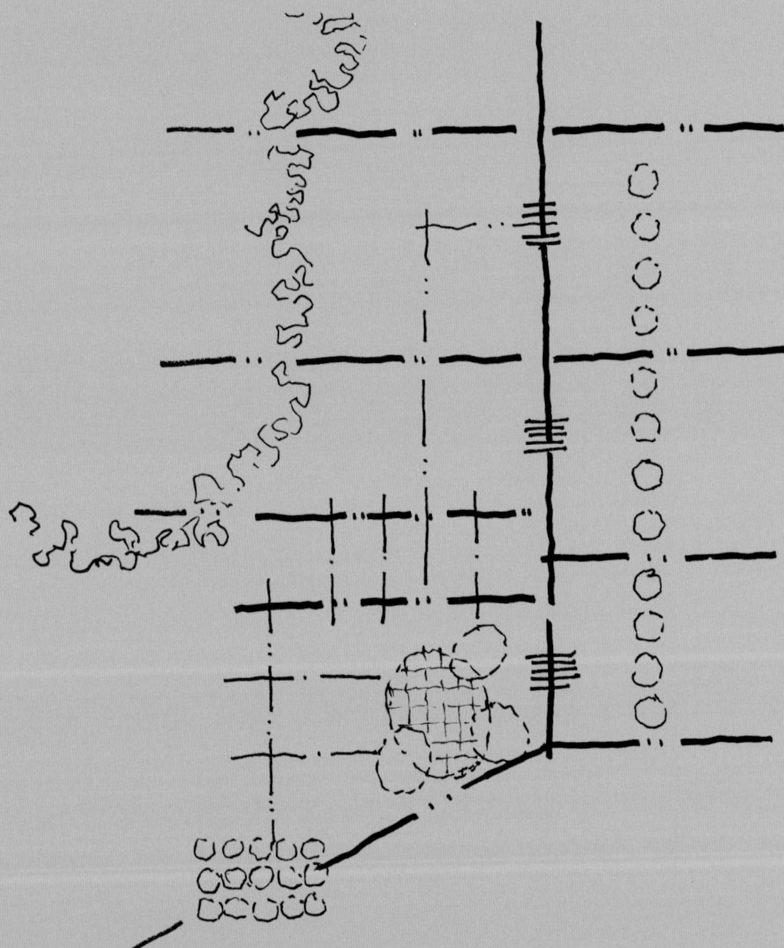

FULLERTON FRESHMAN CAMPUS

Location	Fullerton, California
Latitude/Longitude	33°52'59.4"N 117°52'58.6"W
Client	State of California
Date	2008–11
Size	348,000 sq ft
Awards	California Higher Education Sustainability Conference, Best Sustainable Design, 2010 Green Building Council LEED, Platinum Rating, 2012

The Telltale Fountain

On entering a soaring stone cathedral for the first time, we are likely to receive the message the architect intended: you are small, you should feel humble; this vast space is the home of something powerful. Early movie palaces conveyed an equally clear message: for a small amount of money, for at least a few hours, you will be entertained as if you were royalty. Similarly, an old-fashioned chrome-laden diner sent the message (after the 1918 pandemic): "We're clean and free of germs. You can eat safely here."

All seriously designed architecture is trying to tell us something. We don't even need to know explicitly what that message is. Somehow, almost invisibly, we sense that we are being told where to go and, to some extent, how we should feel.

Architecture tells us how to use it with its own silent language. Instead of words, we sense intention: "Go here," or "Pause here and reflect," or "Here is the entrance you are looking for." If we learn to "read" that language, we begin to become literate in architecture. And, with that skill, we can better understand the world we're living in, and, if the architect is clever, understand their wit and even their jokes.

California State University at Fullerton (CSUF) is a large, mostly commuter campus in Southern California. Over the past few decades, leadership has been shifting the culture of the campus, building several waves of dormitories to attract full-time students and give rise to a vibrant round-the-clock environment.

The second of these dormitory projects was designed for freshmen. For these young people, living away from home for the first time, the university wanted to be sure they had opportunities to form strong bonds with their peers, to feel wanted and cared for, and to be well supervised.

CSUF also wanted the new dormitories to be closely integrated with the teaching environment and with some administration functions. This would provide the Freshman Campus with its own integrity, including teaching spaces and a dining facility intended to serve both academic and residential users. Lastly, the university wanted the students to be aware that their new home was at the forefront of environmental leadership.

ABOVE THE LEED PLATINUM AWARD FOR BEST ENVIRONMENTAL PRACTICES, AFFIXED TO A COMMONS BUILDING ENTRANCE.

RIGHT THE NEW CALIFORNIA STATE UNIVERSITY AT FULLERTON FRESHMAN CAMPUS (IN WHITE).

ANSWER 1

The journey is as important as the destination.

QUESTION 1

How did we integrate the potentially isolated Freshman Campus with the existing residential and academic cores?

CLUE:
RED LINES SHOW WHERE PEOPLE CAN WALK

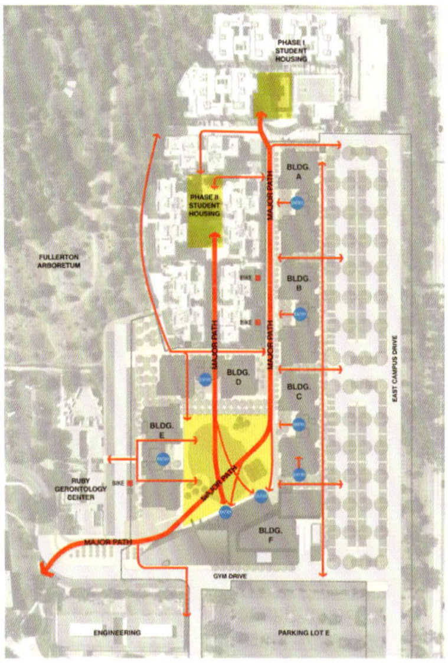

CLUE:
VARIOUS WAYS IN LEAD TO THE CENTRAL PIAZZA

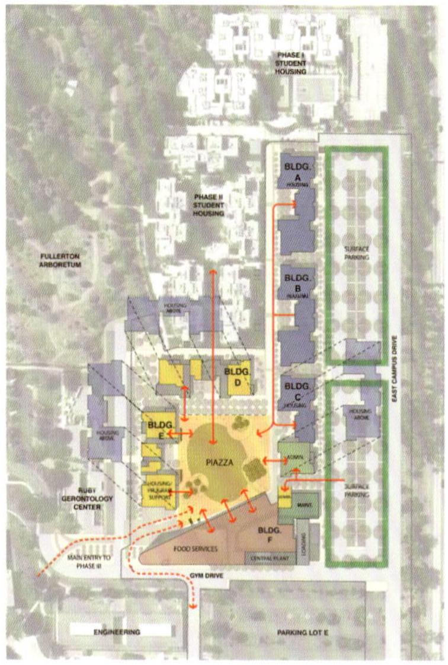

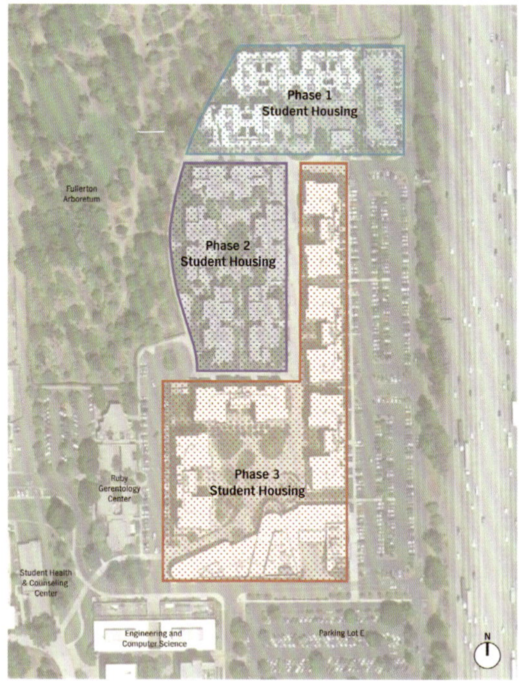

CLUE:
PHASE 3 IS THE FRESHMAN CAMPUS, AND THE ACADEMIC CORE OF THE CAMPUS BEGINS AT 7:00 (LOWER LEFT)

QUESTION 2

How did we create outdoor spaces that work for large and small groups, and even individuals?

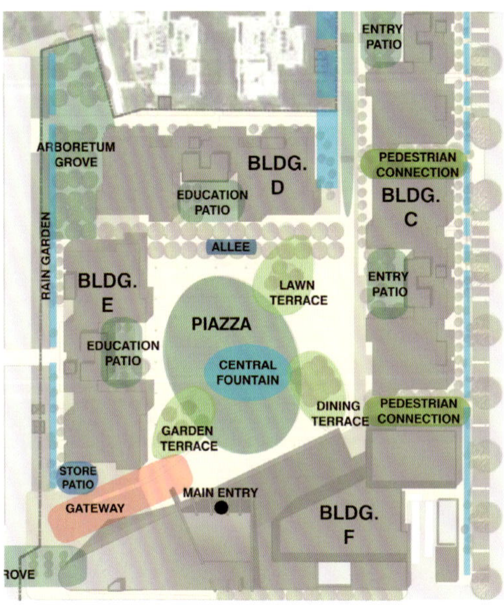

CLUE:
LAWN TERRACE

CLUE:
GARDEN TERRACE

CLUE:
DINING TERRACE

QUESTION 3

For the piazza we had a budget for 60 trees. How did we get the most bang for our buck?

CLUE:
LANDSCAPE PLAN

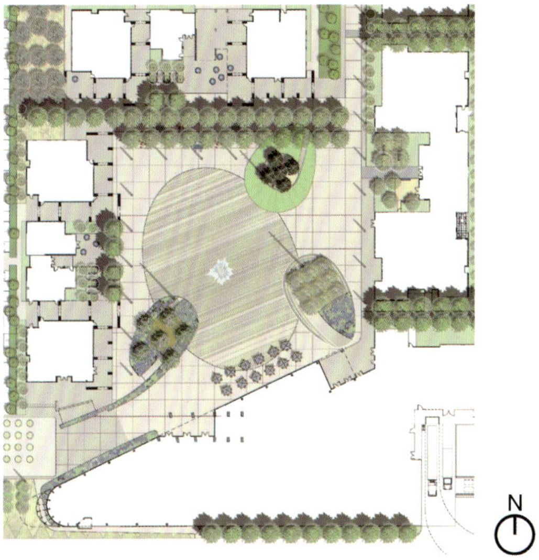

CLUE:
LOW AND HIGH LANDSCAPE

QUESTION 4

How did we demonstrate the university's commitment to sustainability?

CLUE:
THE FOUNTAIN'S HEIGHT CHANGES THROUGHOUT THE DAY

CLUE:
AT THE CENTER OF THE PIAZZA, A FOUNTAIN

ANSWER 3

The trees are positioned to provide multiple effects: the rows of trees on the sunny side of the piazza offer shade, soften the height of the five-story buildings, and provide enclosure for outdoor learning spaces.

ANSWER 2

Smaller-scale spaces give students an opportunity to discover a favorite spot of their own.

ANSWER 4

The volume of the fountain increases and decreases in reverse proportion to the utilization of water by the students.

ANSWER 5

It is easy to understand where your room is.

QUESTION 5

The basic dorm room module was repeated 1,200 times. How did we make the dorms feel like home?

CLUE:
A SINGLE DORM ROOM

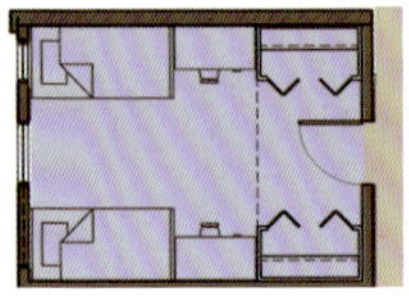

CLUE:
FOUR DORM ROOMS AND THEIR BATHROOM

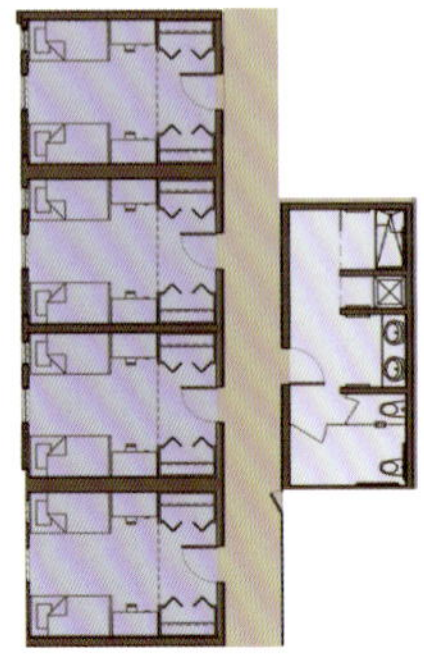

CLUE:
A PINWHEEL OF 12 DORM ROOMS

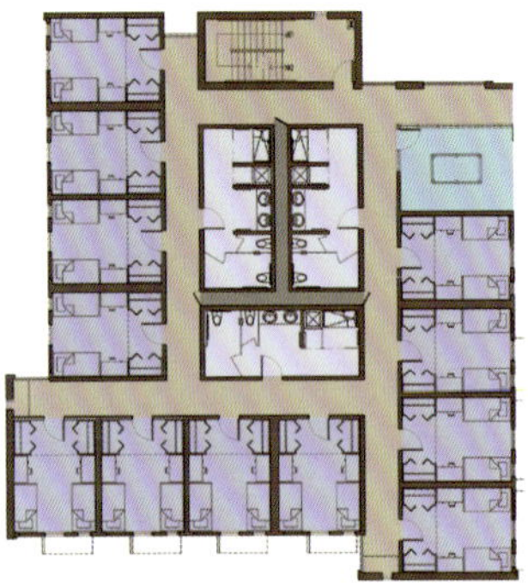

CLUE:
A FULL FLOOR OF 24 ROOMS WITH COMMON SPACES IN BETWEEN

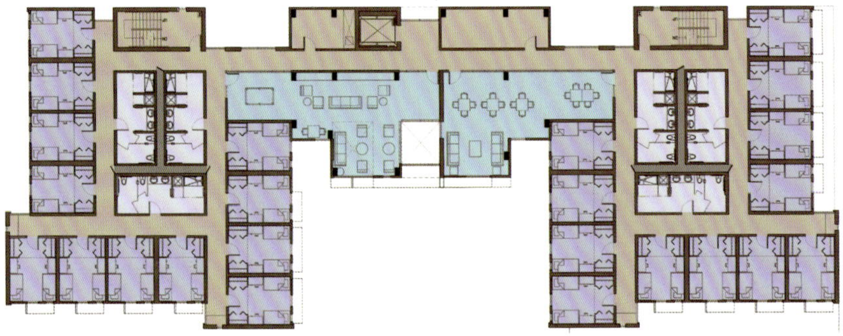

QUESTION 6

How does architecture control visual noise?

CLUE:
DORM ROOMS

CLUE:
COMMONS

CLUE:
DORM ROOMS

QUESTION 7

How did the architecture make communal spaces inviting and encourage participation by new students?

CLUE:
THE ENTRY

CLUE:
COMMUNAL SPACES

QUESTION 8

How did the architecture make a freshman's first home away from home, shared with two other students, more personal?

CLUE:
ONE WINDOW, AS REQUIRED BY CODE, ILLUMINATES THE FLOOR

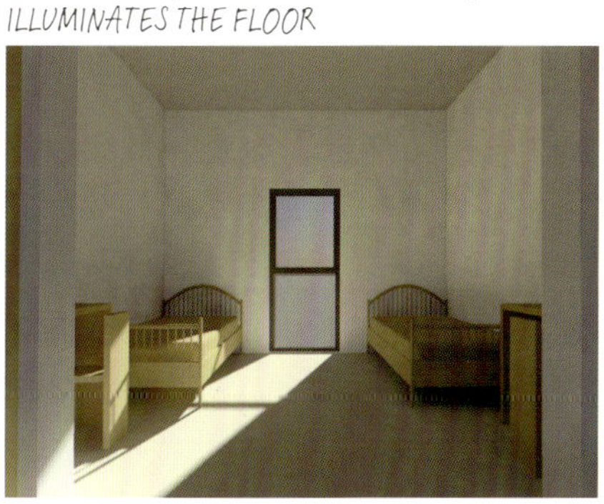

CLUE:
TWO WINDOWS EXPAND THE SPACE BY WASHING THE WALL

CLUE:
THREE WINDOWS BALANCE THE LIGHT

ANSWER 6

Large neutral surfaces provide visual pauses.

ANSWER 7

The lofty entry beckons, and the common spaces promote a playful opportunity to make connections.

ANSWER 8

For either two or three people, the dorms have a unique window for each person.

Emergency

ANSWER 9

The other rooms and spaces are private. This building, the Gastrodome, is a public gathering space.

QUESTION 9
Why is the shape of this building so different from all the others?

CLUE:
THE FLOORPLAN

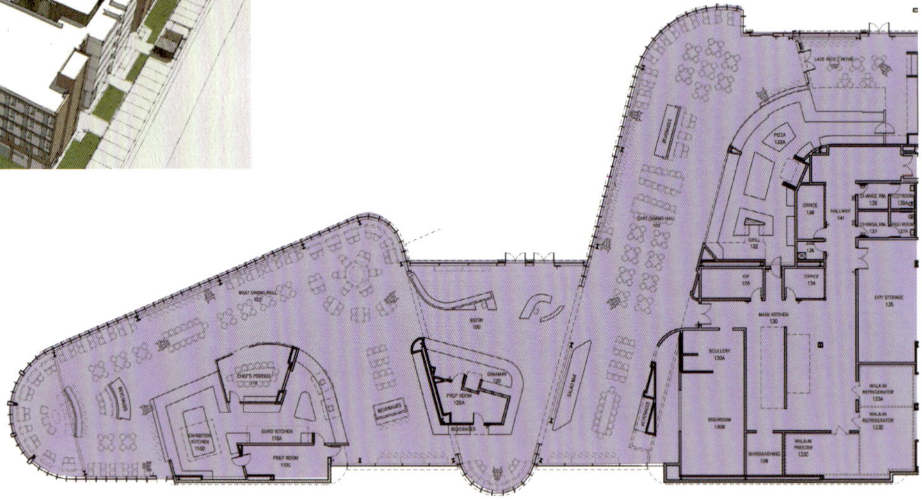

QUESTION 10
How can architecture create an invitation to the outside academic campus to come and visit the Freshman Campus?

CLUE:
THE GASTRODOME AS SEEN FROM THE ACADEMIC CAMPUS, SHOWING EXTENSIVE USE OF GLASS

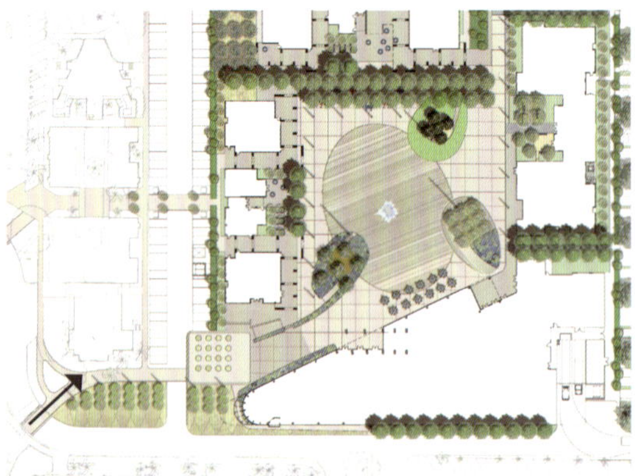

CLUE:
FROM THE ACADEMIC CAMPUS

QUESTION 11

If the top of the windows were a straight line, what would be lost?

QUESTION 12

How can architecture make the Gastrodome an authentic part of the larger community?

ANSWER 11

A. **The transition from the academic campus would be too abrupt. With the curves and shift in window heights, the Gastrodome points us toward the entrance.**

B. **At night, the transparency of the Gastrodome creates a beacon to the outside world.**

ANSWER 10

A. **The building on the left is more solid, while the Gastrodome is open and dynamic, different in height and materials.**

B. **The use of a vanishing point funnel, draws people to the Gastrodome.**

ANSWER 12

The Gastrodome evokes an auto-centric culture, where most people feel a connection with the drive-ins of the past.

7 ARCHITECTURE IS ART

Architecture goes beyond the utilitarian skill of responding to physical and functional requirements. Elevating the spirit through rebellious exploration, it provides new perspectives on the known, allowing others to see things differently.

PRIVATE RESIDENCE	
Location	Atherton, California
Latitude/Longitude	37°26'45.7"N 122°12'26.2"W
Client	Private
Date	1992–96
Size	7,900 sq ft

REAR YARD TOWARD LIVING ROOM

REAR YARD TOWARD LIBRARY

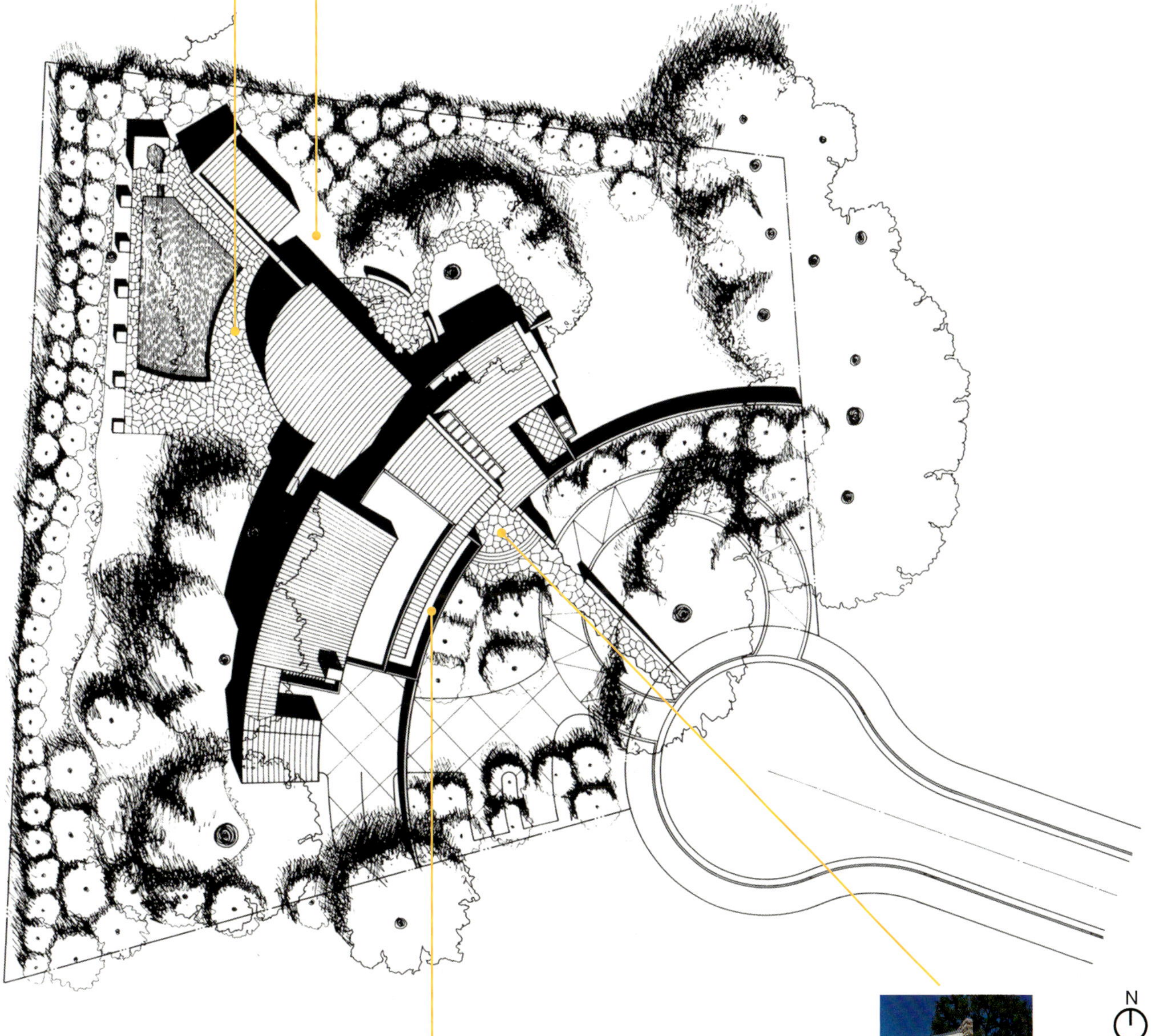

FRONT ENTRY

BALCONY OVERLOOKING FRONT ENTRY

MASTER BEDROOM TERRACE

LIBRARY

MASTER BEDROOM, DOOR RETRACTED

LIVING ROOM

LIVING ROOM WITH FRONT DOOR REAR LEFT

THE WALL

DINING ROOM

KITCHEN/FAMILY SPACE

COLIN POWELL
Kobbé's Complete Opera Book

UPSTAIRS OFFICE

BRIDGE TO OFFICE

STAIRCASE

STREET VIEW, ORIGIN OF WALL ON LEFT

NOTES FROM THE ARTIST

The commission began at the request of a patron, but in my imagination I was designing the house as if for myself.

One arrived at the property via a winding road through a mature forest. At the very end, the property itself began. The lot was a trapezoid — narrow in front and splaying out to the rear. The front of the house was not a straight line, but a curve that matched the *cul-de-sac*. The arced front wall echoed that curve, embracing the visitor.

The site offered three elements that inspired me: four majestic Valley Oaks, the remnants of old stone walls scattered throughout the site, and a creek at the far end. The thick bark of the oaks provided a rich, earthy palette; the stones called out to be reimagined; and the creek offered a resolution to the journey.

I chose materials that harmonized with what I was given: two woods, two stones, and a metal.
RTS

8 ARCHITECTURE REQUIRES LEADERSHIP

Architecture requires leadership that can develop a clear vision, build consensus, and sustain that vision over time.

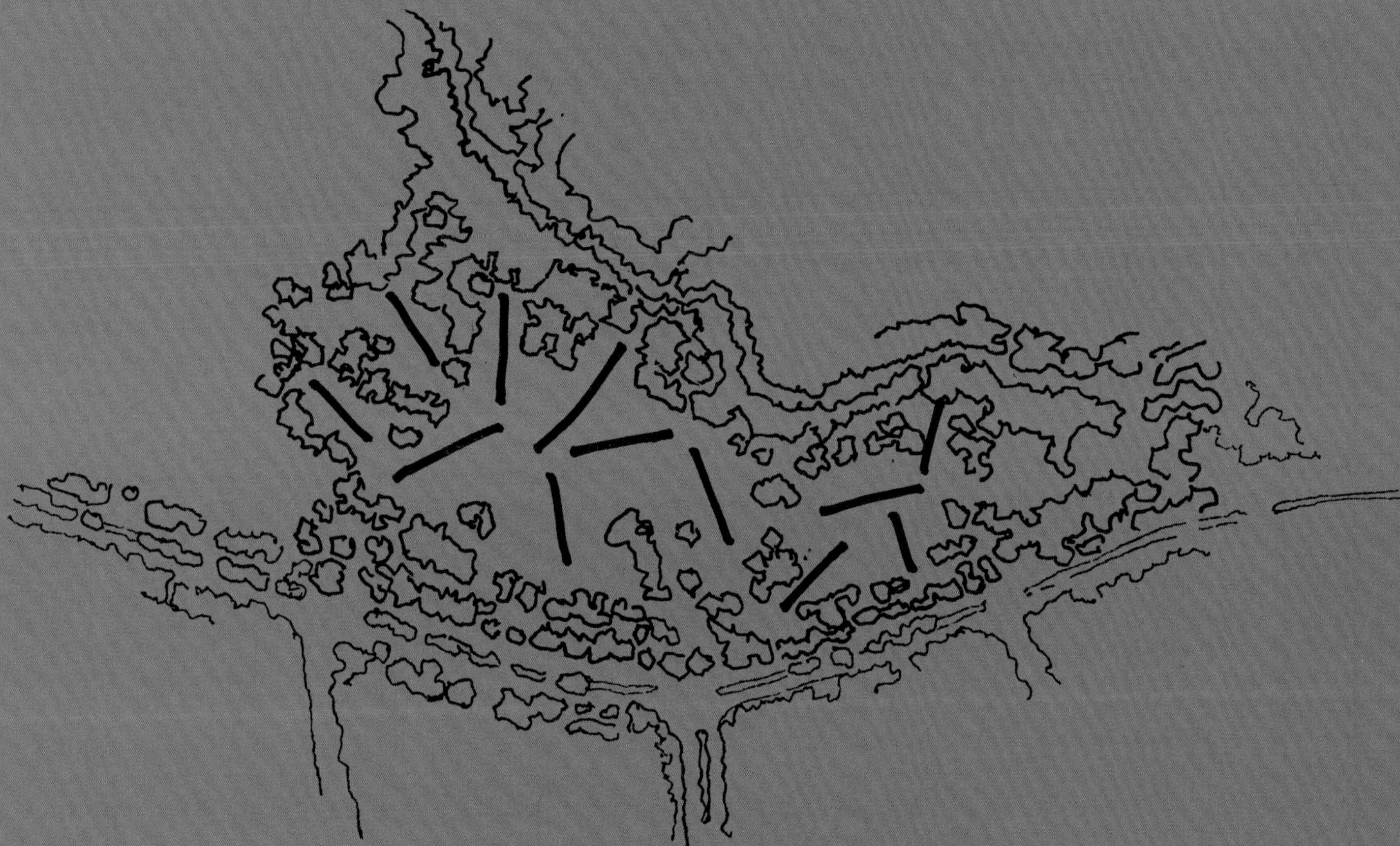

CRBH — THE VI	
Location	Stanford, California
Latitude/Longitude	37°26'25.4"N 122°10'35.0"W
Client	Classic Residences by Hyatt
Date	1986–2006
Size	1,000,000 sq ft
Awards	2005 McGraw Hill, Best of California
	2005 National Association of Home Builders, Gold & Silver Awards, best large CCRC
	2006 Pacific Coast Builders' Conference/Builder Magazine, Grand Award/Senior Housing

RECIPROCITY

To attract young faculty members, Stanford University offers tenure-track professors the opportunity to buy a subsidized home on campus. By the early 1980s the problem for Stanford was that there was a limited supply of these on-campus homes, and there were lots of retired faculty occupying many of them. What to do? Build a large senior housing project so irresistible to the retirees that they would abandon their houses, freeing them up for a new wave of young faculty.

In those days, every week or so, my wife, Alice, and I visited my parents in their elegant home in Los Altos Hills for dinner. As time went on, the house seemed to loom ever larger, and they, with all of us children gone, seemed to be just a tiny bit more vulnerable. My father was stepping back from the firm, finishing what would be his final architectural projects.

I realized I had a vision of the new home that I wanted to create for them, and I began to track the Stanford project.

TOP THE LELAND STANFORD HOME, *C.*1880.

RIGHT THE 25-ACRE SITE, BORDERED BY SAND HILL ROAD, PALO ALTO, TO THE SOUTH AND SAN FRANCISQUITO CREEK, MENLO PARK, TO THE NORTH.

THE FIRST VISION: A CONTINUING CARE RETIREMENT COMMUNITY (CCRC)

Stanford's initial vision in 1982 was for a 1,500-unit residential project. A full year later, the City of Palo Alto came back with an approval for 1,200 units. Stanford refused to accept Palo Alto's proposal, citing the current bottlenecks on Sand Hill Road that no one wanted to pay to improve.

Three short years later, Stanford approved a 600-unit apartment complex that was to become part of the existing Stanford West Apartments, with 12 acres reserved as an archaeological preserve to recognize the ground once occupied by the Muwekma Ohlone people.

I had been building a national reputation as an architect who understood how to make senior housing of all kinds work both aesthetically and financially. I began to build my team, partnering with a senior-housing operator and a contractor to create Sand Hill Partners.

By the end of 1987, when Stanford said yes to our team's proposal, I was clear who my target market was: my parents and 700 or so of their closest friends. We envisioned creating a Continuing Care Retirement Community (CCRC). The financial arrangement for CCRCs generally anticipates a partially refundable ownership interest in the property and monthly fees for various services.

The ultimate site was 25 of the choicest acres on the Stanford campus. It had been so perfect that Governor Leland Stanford had chosen to build his own home on it and raise his family there. The site's heritage went back at least five millennia and well before the Spanish first set foot in California, when the Muwekma Ohlone people had settled along the creeks and rivers around the San Francisco Bay area. Eventually the Spanish missionaries began to develop agriculture in the region until, in 1876, Governor Stanford purchased 8,180 bucolic acres in what is now Palo Alto.

When we began walking the site it still boasted more than 400 live oaks, and a gurgling, meandering creek. For our future residents, the Stanford Medical Center was close by, and the best shopping in the region — at the Stanford Shopping Center — was across the street.

There were just a few little wrinkles to smooth out, and then we could start building. Or so we hoped.

1982

Stanford proposes concept for 1,500-unit residential project

The Equal Rights Amendment to the U.S. Constitution fails to gain ratification. Feminists are frustrated

Israel invades Lebanon to attack the PLO, the Palestine Liberation Organization

The U.K. defeats Argentina in a war over the isolated Falkland Islands

The Vietnam Memorial opens in Washington

1983

City of Palo Alto approves a 1,200-unit residential project BUT Stanford refuses to accept due to Sand Hill Road conditions

Astronaut Sally Ride becomes the first American woman in space

President Reagan announces his plans for a missile defense plan called Star Wars

A terrorist explosion in Beirut kills 237 U.S. Marines

1984

Indian Prime Minister Indira Gandhi is assassinated

Apple introduces the Macintosh personal computer

OPPOSITE THE SITE WITH 12 ACRES OF ARCHAEOLOGICAL PRESERVE AND HUNDREDS OF MATURE TREES.

THE BLACK GOWN

The Stanford administration was a vast bureaucracy, carefully nursing its substantial endowment, and burnishing its prestige. It also protected itself by becoming what I can only describe as an obscure authority system. We never knew with whom we were dealing. A project manager would come to us with a problem to be solved. We would create what we felt was the best solution, or even develop multiple alternatives. The manager would disappear to gather data and study the issue, and eventually return with an edict from behind the black gown. We never learned who was behind that curtain. Was it one person? A committee of fifteen? And of course, dealing with imaginary authority, we were always trying to figure out whether there was any pattern to their thinking. Over the years we gave up trying. We couldn't manage something we couldn't control.

THE GOLDEN TOWN

The City of Palo Alto has a love-hate bond with its great university. Locals acknowledge Stanford's contribution to the city's cultural and economic vitality, its impact on a successful public-school district, and its prominent role in sustaining healthy home prices. But Palo Alto had been decidedly hostile to development in general, and suspicious of Stanford's ever-growing vision of itself as not only a global university but also as the major health center in the region. Stanford had the money, and land, and the desire to grow prodigiously.

With a passion for individualism, resistance to gentrification, and a strong desire to retain its culture, Palo Alto had established a notoriously arduous zoning approval process designed to discourage development. A development the size and scope of Stanford's sweeping proposal, was not warmly embraced by the city.

THE NECESSARY EXPERTS

Being sophisticated stewards of the environment, Stanford and Palo Alto liked to compete over how many experts they could bring to the table to oversee any development. From my earliest days on the project, I found myself attempting to find common ground between our design team, the Native American advocates, business experts, arborists, archaeologists, and many others who felt it their duty to impose further requirements on the project. Each requirement caused a cascade of effects. Our design flexibility was increasingly narrowed, each requirement inevitably took something away from another constituent, and resolving each development pushed the project back another week, or month, or year. Or even more.

Arborists

The arborists evaluated, numbered, tagged, and made recommendations for each of the 600 trees on the site. They even gave names to their favorites. The goal of this work was the protection and preservation of each native oak, redwood, and the historically significant Governor's Row, an avenue of eucalyptus trees linking the academic campus with the proposed new senior living community. The result of their work, ultimately, became the framework of where we could place the one million square feet of building. And in a few instances, we repositioned the massive oaks.

Archaeologist

The university archaeologist, who carried a whistle, wielded the authority to stop the project

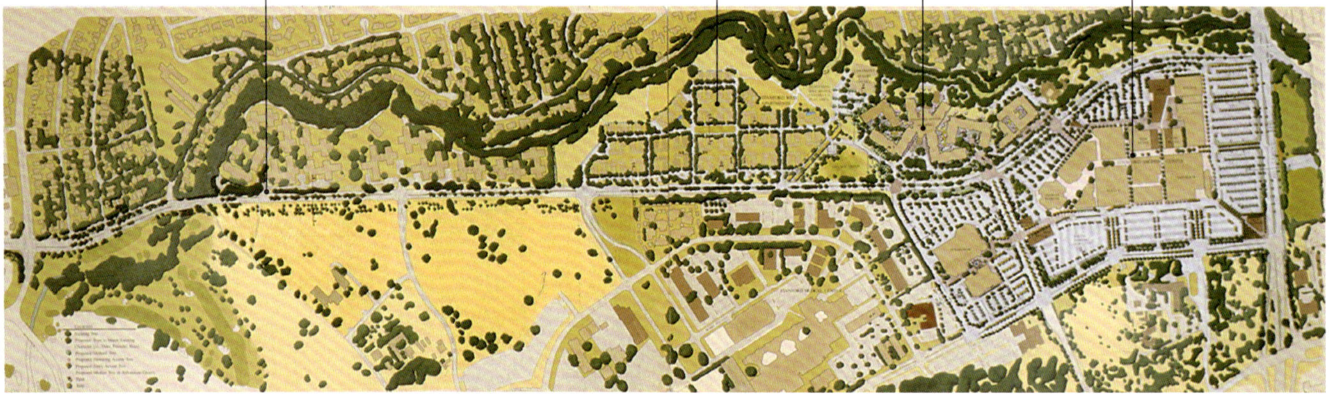

at any time simply by identifying a fragment or artifact of the Leland Stanford family's time on the site. She scoured the site morning and night looking for items of interest to the university's Special Collections department. Her discoveries had the potential to change previously approved design plans: if she found a new spoon, we might have to relocate a five-story building 10 feet or more. When she blew her whistle, everything stopped. Although we became friends, I was scared to death when my phone rang and her name appeared on the screen.

The Ohlone People

The Native American tribes associated with the memory of the Ohlone People's settlement along the river inside the proposed site put forth various advocates to address some of the complex mysteries yet remaining under the soil. A second staff of historians and archaeologists was soon attached to the project, and we were well aware that they too could stop us at any moment, even when we got to construction.

Early on the city dictated that we respect substantial archaeological building setbacks of 150 feet from the creek bank to avoid disturbing Native American burial sites. This meant that we were precluded from building on a huge portion of the site, which significantly affected our design. Despite our respectful efforts in advance of construction, the site was nevertheless shut down more than a dozen times. When we encountered Ohlone remains, everything came to a screeching halt as Native American elders were summoned to perform ritual dances, chants and ceremonies, and smoke the tribal pipe. It was an awe-inspiring sight to behold the first time it happened, and even the second and third time. But by the 10th, and now pushing against rigid timelines imposed by Stanford, Palo Alto, and even Hyatt, these interruptions were beginning to lose their charm.

The Creek and the Water District

The San Francisquito Creek that had delighted Leland Stanford a hundred and fifty years before was not only a creek, a burial site, and an archaeological dig, it was also home to protected frogs, and was itself a potential bringer of floods. The Santa Clara County Water District decided that we needed to build our foundations a few feet above grade. The Palo Alto city planning

1986

Stanford approves concept for a 600-unit residential project with a 12-acre archaeological preserve

An explosion in the nuclear power plant at Chernobyl in the USSR spreads radiation over Russia and Europe

Nintendo introduces the hand-held Game Boy

1987

Stanford approves concept for the redevelopment of Old Children's Hospital for 330 units of faculty housing and 450 units of senior housing

1988

Sand Hill Partners selected to develop senior's project

George Bush elected U.S. President

1989

In China, more than a million demonstrate in Tiananmen Square for more democracy

Berlin Wall falls

department insisted we bury the buildings lower into the ground in order to meet height restrictions. I was the ping-pong ball swatted back and forth.

The creek was also, unfortunately for us, a border. On our side was Palo Alto; across the creek was the wealthy and conservative town of Menlo Park. Solutions to every challenge to do with the creek required agreement between the Native Americans, the County Water District, the cities of Palo Alto and Menlo Park, and the landowner, Stanford University.

While Stanford had plenty of experience and expertise in real-estate development, the university had never before pursued a senior housing project. As my Stanford colleagues evolved their understanding of the complexities of the economic, operational, and social dimensions of senior housing, they continually rethought the model, tossing all the pieces in the air to be reassembled in different configurations.

With each of these changes in fundamental strategy, four times in 18 years, Stanford decided they needed to recruit new advisors. Someone whispered in their ear, planting the seeds of doubt, and they would loose confidence in their current consultants. With each change, our team scrambled in a new direction.

With each change, my job was to provide continuity, to bring the new advisor up to speed on the history of the project, to referee challenges to decisions already established, and to recast the vision for one million square feet of space that ultimately would include one-, two-, and

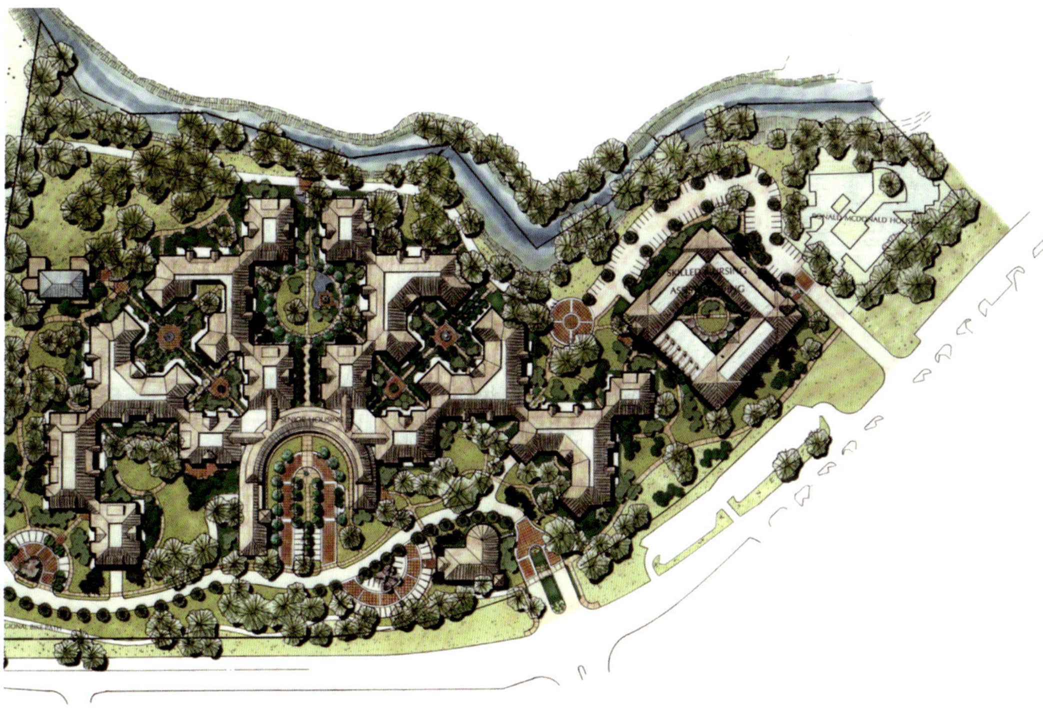

OPPOSITE COMPOSITE PLAN OF THE FOUR PROPOSED PROJECTS.

BELOW INITIAL VISION FOR SENIOR HOUSING.

1990

Nelson Mandela is freed after 27 years as a political prisoner in South Africa

1991

The U.S. and allies win the Persian Gulf War against Iraq

1992

Introduction of consolidated projects to City of Palo Alto AND termination of development agreement with Sand Hill Partners

Bill Clinton is elected President of the United States

1993

Nokia sends text messages between mobile phones

1994

Football star O. J. Simpson is arrested for the killings of his wife and her friend Ronald Goldman

Amazon.com is born

1995

Sony demonstrates a flat-screen TV

1997

Palo Alto City Council entitlement approval for Sand Hill Road, Stanford Shopping Center, Stanford West Apartments and Senior housing

Princess Diana is killed with two others in a Paris car crash

J. K. Rowling publishes the first Harry Potter book

OPPOSITE THREE SKETCHES FOR THE INITIAL VISION.

three-bedroom units, five penthouses, assisted living, memory care, skilled nursing, multiple restaurants, and recreation facilities.

INITIAL VISION, EVENTUALLY SCRAPPED

The proposed senior living community at Stanford originated as part of a bundle of unrelated projects along the Sand Hill Road corridor. Noted for the prominent venture capital firms dotting the three-mile stretch from Interstate 280 to the Stanford Shopping Center, Sand Hill Road was notorious as a main artery that came to an abrupt, dead-end in the mall's parking lot. In a nutshell, Stanford agreed to pay for some $20 million Sand Hill Road improvements — including its extension to El Camino Real — in exchange for City approval of three projects: a 628-unit development of rental housing to be occupied by graduate students and young faculty; an 80,000-square-foot addition to the Stanford Shopping Center; and our project, the senior living community.

THE SECOND VISION: OWNERSHIP AND RENTAL

By the fall of 1992, the City demanded Stanford consolidate their four mammoth projects into one development proposal for the City to consider. Gone was my team, Sand Hill Partners. They were paid off, and I remained as the architect for the senior housing project.

Stanford also changed their mind about the financial strategy for the project. Out was the notion of seniors buying in (the CCRC model), and instead Stanford envisioned a hybrid, with one-half rental and one-half ownership. For me, this meant a major redesign. And we needed to go back to all constituencies: my friends at the City of Palo Alto, my archaeologists and my arborists.

Stanford stayed with their hybrid plan for two years, giving me enough time to get most of the major planning work finished again, and to achieve buy-in from my many conflicting forces, each of which took the opportunity to attempt to claw back what they may have previously bargained away.

THE THIRD VISION: RENTAL

Then after a couple of years getting comfortable with their hybrid proposal, the leadership at Stanford began to feel less comfortable with their vision. A new consultant had now advised that an all-rental model was a really good idea. Once again, I needed to run revisions to all constituencies, giving them a heads-up as to our latest pivot, and prepare for the three government entities whose approval we required.

Ultimately, the final package agreed to by Stanford and the City of Palo Alto included the following elements:

- Stanford would pay for and implement more than $20 million in roadway improvements in the Sand Hill corridor that would significantly improve circulation in that area and simultaneously reduce traffic in nearby neighborhoods.
- Stanford would be allowed to construct 628 rental housing units on the Stanford West site.
- The site of Leland Stanford's house would be redeveloped into my Senior Housing Community, with 388 independent-living units, 60 assisted-living units, 24 memory-care units and 45 skilled-nursing beds.
- The shopping center would be permitted to increase by 80,000 square feet.
- Stanford would lease park land to the City and agreed to set aside 139 acres along Sand Hill Road for open space.

The City's response was encouraging but noncommittal. Stanford concluded that the entire package contained many substantial benefits that would result in citizen support in the community and could probably win the approval of the Palo Alto City Council. But it was also acknowledged that there would be determined opposition and a high likelihood that any approval would end up on the ballot and, if passed, opponents would likely launch a lawsuit. At that point, the City estimated that a final decision would take two years.

In reality, it took five years to reach the ballot stage.

After intensive work between Stanford and City staff, the Palo Alto City Council held the longest and largest series of hearings in Palo Alto history — eight months, twenty-one full, open sessions — to take testimony from more than 1,000 Palo Alto and Menlo Park residents to deliberate on these projects. My job was to speak, to show drawings, illustrations, and charts that would leverage the senior housing, which everyone agreed on, in order to get approvals for expanded roadways and increased commercial square footage.

The Council instructed the City Manager to insist on further modifications to the university's application. We redesigned our projects and submitted revised applications in the fall of 1994. The final Environmental Impact Report for our projects was published in eight volumes — the most intense and thorough review of any project in the history of Palo Alto.

In final consideration of the revised package, the Council voted unanimously (9–0), to approve the projects and signed a development agreement the size of a small telephone book.

This appeared to be a happy ending. But the

1998

Letter of intent signed by Hyatt and Stanford

Google introduces its search engine to the Web

1999

Old Children's Hospital demolished

The Y2K Scare raises the possibility that databases all over the world would go haywire

2000

Ground lease signs with Hyatt

In one of the closest, contested elections on record, George W. Bush defeats Al Gore for President

The human genome sequence is deciphered opening new possibilities in medicine

High prices for Internet company stocks tumble as the "Dot-Com Bubble" bursts

2001

On September 11, terrorists attack the World Trade Center in New York

Half of all Americans now use the Internet

Apple's iPod becomes the bestselling MP3 player in the world

2002

City of Palo Alto Architectural Review Board approves 388 independent living units, 38 one-bedroom assisted-living units, 24 memory-impaired units and a 44-room skilled-nursing facility

OPPOSITE ABOVE SITE PLAN FOR THE SECOND VISION SHOWING THE TWO LOBBIES.

OPPOSITE BELOW RENDERING FOR THE SECOND VISION.

story was not over. The City of Menlo Park sued the City of Palo Alto and Stanford, claiming the eight-volume environmental review was still inadequate.

We were also concerned that there might be a referendum put to the public to get a vote on the project, and we were aware that one group or another might get enough signatures to put an initiative on the ballot that would attempt to kill the project.

We got both. The City Council put the Development Agreement on the ballot for the voters' approval. Opponents of the projects gained enough signatures for an initiative that was a thinly disguised poison pill to stop the development. Ultimately, Palo Alto voters overwhelmingly backed the university's plan and rejected the initiative.

We believed we were in a position to break ground.

Except we didn't. Stanford was getting increasingly uncomfortable with their own ability to manage all of these different kinds of real-estate projects. They were especially concerned about operating the highly specialized kind of project that would house, feed, and care for an aging population of seniors.

THE FOURTH VISION: AN OUTSIDE DEVELOPER AND MANAGER

Stanford began a search for a partner firm with expertise in developing and managing continuing care senior communities. Stanford asked me if any of the senior housing developers we had worked with would be a good candidate for operating partner.

Fortunately, I had been laying the groundwork for this question for some time. My close friend, Penny Pritzker, was one of the nation's leading experts on senior housing development and management, having founded Classic Residences by Hyatt in 1987 and had already purchased or developed a number of highly regarded senior living projects. Penny would bring the highest level of operational know-how to the premier senior living community Stanford envisioned.

In August, 1998, Penny Pritzker and Stanford signed a deal to create Classic Residences by Hyatt at Stanford. We were going to build 500 residences in a continuing care retirement community for seniors, and Penny's organization would operate the community.

I was delighted and relieved. For at least a week, I celebrated the fact that I was no longer alone, that things would go smoothly, that our mutual vision would finally be realized.

Not only was Penny a dual-degree holder from Stanford (Law and Business) she also coupled the experience of operating other senior communities with her experience in the hospitality industry. I had no doubt that she and her team would ensure efficient operations and deliver the highest level of service.

Because of our close family relationship and our shared experience growing up in homes designed by my father, Penny instantly understood my vision for the community and supported it wholeheartedly. She allowed me almost unlimited autonomy. Her confidence in me, combined with her operational and hospitality knowledge made for a complementary and constructive partnership.

Being a leader sometimes means letting others lead. Penny's team helped us evaluate complex issues that required balancing trade-offs between up-front costs and long-term, operational costs. For example, we debated

THE DESIGN TEAM LEADS ONE OF TWO WEEKEND-LONG COMMUNITY-WIDE CHARETTES.

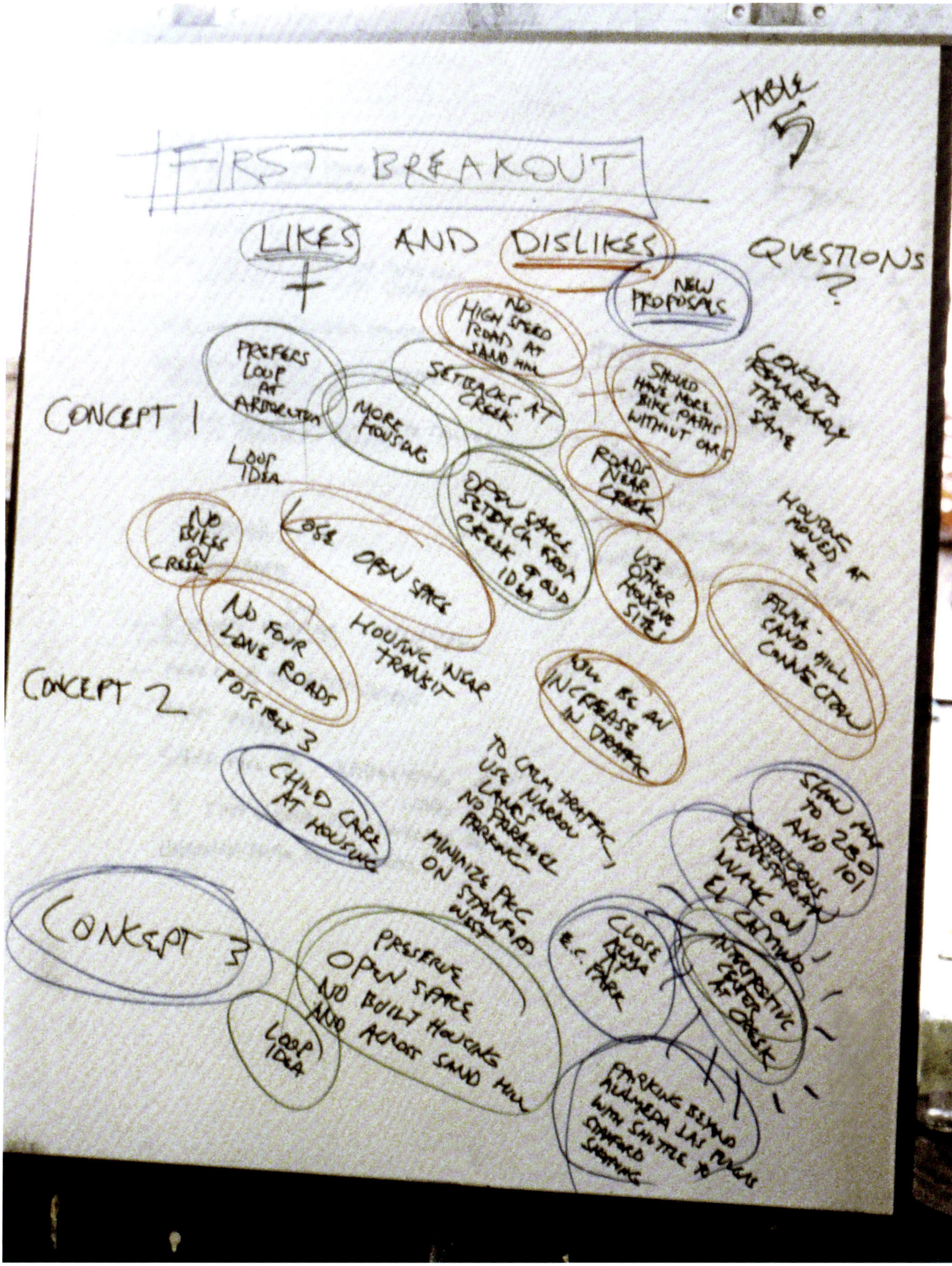
FIRST BREAKOUT
TABLE 5
LIKES +
AND
DISLIKES
QUESTIONS ?
NEW PROPOSALS
NO HIGH SPEED ROAD AT SAND HILL
PREFERS LOOP AT ARBORETUM
SETBACKS AT CREEK
SHOULD HAVE MORE BIKE PATHS WITHOUT CARS
CONCEPTS REMARKABLY THE SAME
CONCEPT 1
MORE HOUSING
LOOP IDEA
ROADS NEAR CREEK
OPEN SPACE SETBACK FROM CREEK GOOD IDEA
NO BIKES ON CREEK
LOSE OPEN SPACE
HOUSING MOVED AT #2
USE OTHER HOUSING SITES
NO FOUR LANE ROADS
HOUSING NEAR TRANSIT
ALMA - SAND HILL CONNECTION
CONCEPT 2
POSSIBLY 3
WILL BE AN INCREASE IN TRAFFIC
CHILD CARE AT HOUSING
TO CALM TRAFFIC USE NARROW LANES NO PARALLEL PARKING
SHOW MAP TO 280 AND 101
CONTINUOUS PEDESTRIAN WALK ON EL CAMINO
MINIMIZE REC ON STANFORD WEST
CONCEPT 3
PRESERVE OPEN SPACE NO BUILT HOUSING AND ACROSS SAND HILL
CLOSE ALMA AT E.C. PARK
INTERPRETIVE CENTER AT CREEK
LOOP IDEA
PARKING BEYOND ALAMEDA LAS PULGAS WITH SHUTTLE TO STANFORD SHOPPING

whether to build one or two kitchens to serve two separate buildings with varying levels of care and different dietary requirements. In the end, we built one upgraded kitchen that had higher up-front costs, but only required one team of kitchen staff, saving considerably in ongoing operational expenses. Heated, motorized shuttles would deliver food to the appropriate building.

Tempering Penny's support and freedom, Classic Residences' chief architect monitored and evaluated every recommendation I made. Like a bulldog, he nipped at my trouser leg and would not let go no matter how hard I tried to shake him off. In a pinch, I could make use of my back-channel access to Penny, but I rarely played that card. Over time, he and I developed mutual respect and a constructive collaboration. But at the time, ten years into a project with more overseers than I had ever experienced before, another layer of scrutiny was the last thing I needed.

Now, at long, long last, we were ready to break ground. Except for one last thing.

THE MOLDAW UNITS

Like me, Penny envisioned that many of our parents' friends would find life in the Classic Residences by Hyatt to be elegant, comfortable, and fulfilling. Imagine her shock and surprise when she asked our mutual family friend and my high school mentor, Stuart Moldaw whether he planned to buy a unit. His immediate answer? "No."

Stuart would be coming from his vast Atherton home, which my father had designed, with live-in help, a catering kitchen, and other amenities that apartment living simply could not support. Stuart felt that even the most spacious of the proposed units would be too confining. Penny called to ask me whether it would be possible to add a unit or two that met Stuart's needs.

On the face of it, this may not seem like a big deal, but adding several penthouse units meant returning to the City of Palo Alto and requesting amendments to the most complicated approvals ever granted in City history. It was akin to escaping a snarling bear and then going back to poke him in the eye. It required new drawings, a new public hearing, and updating and coordinating with all the consultants. Adding this type of unit would set us back months.

But the Moldaws were just the type of residents we wanted to attract, so back to the drawing board we went, referring among ourselves to the five expansive new apartments as "Moldaw Units." The penthouses comprised 5,000 square feet and included all the accoutrements that Stuart had laid out.

Months later, when they finally saw the plans we had created especially for them, the Moldaws said that now they could see the reality of moving in, they just could not do it. So they stayed in their house, and we had five very expensive penthouses to sell.

THE HOME FOR MY PARENTS

I poured my heart and soul into the design of the floorplan I created for my parents, refining every view, every angle, every closet. I considered my mother's love of nature, my father's love of architecture, and the casual, understated, peninsula lifestyle that they and their friends had enjoyed for decades.

However when the Classic Residences finally opened, my father insisted he was "too young" to move into a senior living community. I was absolutely crushed when the unit that

2003

Construction begins

The U.S. and U.K. launch war against Iraq

The space shuttle Columbia explodes killing all seven astronauts

2004

Enormous tsunami devastates Asia. At least 225,000 are killed

George W. Bush is re-elected

Social networking website Facebook takes off

2005

In August, Hurricane Katrina destroys much of the Gulf Coast, flooding New Orleans

London is hit by Islamic terrorist bombings, killing 52 people and wounding 700

The Irish Republican Army announces it is officially ending its violent campaign for a unified Ireland

YouTube posts its first videos

2006

Occupancy

FINAL INDEPENDENT LIVING
SITE PLAN FOR THE CLASSIC
RESIDENCES BY HYATT

I had designed for my parents went to another party. It would be another five years before my parents finally sold their downtown Palo Alto penthouse condominium and moved into the Classic Residences. But they never lived in the apartment that I had custom-designed for them.

IF I KNEW NOW WHAT I KNEW THEN…

Would I do it again? Yes, I would. The Classic Residences by Hyatt were recognized both nationally and internationally as the state-of-the-art senior community. Before long, all the residences were occupied, and the waiting list began to grow — and has never stopped. The building's siting, its integration with the landscape, its plan that fostered social interaction, and the amazingly high level of service that Penny brought to the project all helped make the process of aging in place supportive and dignified. The residents' delight was nearly unanimous.

My parents eventually settled into their new lifestyle, and when I visited many of the residents complemented me. As he got older, Goody walked me around the building, leaning on my arm as he typically did in his later years, and explained the rhythm of the columns, the graceful transition of spaces from one room to another, and the resolution of intersecting forms and materials — as if he had designed it himself! That was his way of acknowledging he was proud of my work. It was the culmination of our thirty-year partnership.

TOP THE AUTHOR'S PARENTS, GOODY AND GERRY STEINBERG.

ABOVE SKETCHES IN RESPONSE TO STANFORD'S REQUIREMENT FOR THE DESIGNS TO REFLECT THE CRAFTSMAN ARCHITECTURE OF THE GREATER COMMUNITY.

THE SPIDER-LIKE SHAPE RESULTED FROM THE NEED TO PRESERVE THE EXISTING TREES BY USING THE FOOTPRINT OF THE ORIGINAL CHILDREN'S HOSPITAL.

620

PREVIOUS SPREAD THE *PORTE-COCHÈRE* REINTERPRETS THE CRAFTSMAN STYLE WOODEN BEAMS WITH STEEL AND STONE, AND PROVIDES THE TRANSITION FROM THE PUBLIC SPACE TO THE PRIVATE RESIDENCES.

OPPOSITE ONE OF THE RESIDENTIAL COURTYARDS. STONE WAS USED TO ADD TEXTURE WHEREVER A RESIDENT MIGHT TOUCH.

RIGHT TOP TO BOTTOM
A BRONZE SCULPTURE OF A MOTHER AND CHILD, COMMISSIONED BY PENNY PRITZKER, RECOGNIZES THE EARLY NATIVE AMERICANS WHO ONCE DWELT ON THE LAND.

AN ACCESSIBLE, SHELTERED OVERLOOK PROVIDES SAFE ACCESS TO THE CREEKSIDE.

THE ZINC AND GLASS FITNESS CENTER, WITH THE JACUZZI AND POOL INSIDE, ENCOURAGES RESIDENTS TO ENJOY THE STARS ABOVE AT NIGHT.

LEFT THE COMMUNITY LIVING ROOM, COMFORTABLE FOR LARGE AND SMALL GATHERINGS.

OPPOSITE ABOVE THE FRONT ENTRANCE AND LOBBY, WITH VIEWS ALL THE WAY THROUGH TO THE CREEK.

OPPOSITE BELOW THE UNIQUE PIECES OF COMMISSIONED ART ARE INTENDED AS WAYFINDING DEVICES TO HELP RESIDENTS NAVIGATE THE FLOORPLAN.

VIEW FROM THE CREEK. FORMAL DINING ON THE RIGHT, LIVING ROOM IN THE MIDDLE AND ARCADE ON THE LEFT.

9 ARCHITECTURE IS INNOVATION

ARCHITECTURE BRINGS IDEAS, CREATIVE THOUGHT, OR IMAGINATION TO ADDRESS EXISTING CONDITIONS, NEW REQUIREMENTS, OR UNARTICULATED NEEDS, RESULTING IN PROGRESS FOR HUMANITY.

CAMPUS FOR JEWISH LIFE	
Location	Palo Alto, California
Latitude/Longitude	37°25'23.9"N 122°06'10.4"W
Client	Taube Koret Campus for Jewish Life
Date	2002–09
Size	435,000 sq ft
Awards	American Institute of Architects / AAHSA, Award of Merit, 2009
	American Institute of Architects, Citation Award, 2010
	American Institute of Architects / Leading Age, Award of Merit, 2011

THE MATCHMAKER AND THE BEACON OF LIGHT

NOTHING BUT OLD PEOPLE

The Stanford University retirement community eventually became recognized as the gold standard for senior residential communities and was featured on the cover of several international books showcasing the "best-of-class" retirement communities from around the world.

And yet something was missing.

One aspect of the project nagged at me. Whenever I visited my parents, I could sense their desire to remain relevant, to connect with a larger cross-section of the community than just their homogenous, senior neighbors. In fact, I heard their hesitation repeatedly. "Gee, there are a lot of old people living here!"

The Palo Alto Jewish Community Center, or JCC, provided the community with a number of services: a preschool, a day camp, senior activities, cultural events, and a fitness program. When the City of Palo Alto notified the JCC that the lease on the facilities they had been renting, a discarded middle-school campus, would not be renewed, leadership of the JCC decided they wanted to establish a permanent home on property they owned. They invited me to join the planning team, to review any site they considered and advise whether it would work.

Competition for sites of any appropriate size was fierce: the tech industry was in full expansion mode, and the Palo Alto real-estate market was overheated. Enter a fading older tech giant: Sun Microsystems. When they put their 12-acre, Palo Alto campus on the market — just off the 101 Freeway, located within minutes of Facebook, Google, and Apple — every local and national developer coveted the property. It was also perfect for the JCC, and although it was too large for its foreseeable needs, it was in close proximity to its current members' homes.

The JCC leadership was determined to somehow make it work. Learning that the Jewish Senior Living Group of San Francisco was also seeking a South Peninsula home, the JCC proposed a partnership to co-occupy the campus, and to raise the funds to build it together. The operators of San Francisco's Jewish Senior Living Group readily agreed.

The JCC made an aggressive bid, much more than it seemed able to afford, and won!

THE SUN MICROSYSTEMS CAMPUS WITH THE SAN FRANCISCO BAY TO THE NORTH. HIGHWAY 101 BORDERS THE SITE.

The two organizations were strange bedfellows, but there was no other way the community would have been able to come up with the funds to make good on the bid. As it turned out, even this partnership was not enough. With the clock ticking toward the day the deal closed, the group reached out to a respected nonprofit residential developer, Bridge Housing, and proposed a joint venture in which the JCC would sell Bridge four of its 12 acres, with an agreement to collaborate to create a coherent new community that would be called the Campus for Jewish Life or CJL.

THE FIRST MARRIAGE

The available time for Bridge to make a decision was inadequate to do a thorough due-diligence analysis of the deal. Fortunately, I had worked for Bridge and had developed very good relationships with its principals and board members. Knowing from my past experience that the board would require some level of site capacity understanding to make the decision to proceed, I proposed to the CJL that I would, at my own expense, develop plans for Bridge to present to its board in an effort to reach an agreement. My stipulation? If Bridge agreed to the proposed partnership, I would be selected as project architect.

At the eleventh hour, Bridge agreed to join the project development team, along with the JCC and the Jewish Senior Living Group. Now the real work began.

The eight-acre remaining parcel to be shared between the JCC and the senior living community required street visibility to attract members; physical separation from the below-market senior housing to be co-located on the campus; surge drop-off, pick-up, and parking for preschool, day camp, cultural arts' presentations, and recreational activities; separate, dedicated parking for residents; and abundant outdoor spaces to complement indoor programming.

THE FIRST VISION

The JCC was clear they needed 150,000 feet of ground-level space for their preschool, their full-scale fitness center, two swimming pools, meeting spaces, cultural spaces, and recreational spaces — all easily accessible. The Jewish Senior Living Group envisioned an 80,000-square-foot stand-alone assisted-living building for their residents. And Bridge Housing was planning for 230 condominiums on the 4-acre site. They looked forward to being close by, so they could benefit from the rich array of services and cultural activities provided by the JCC. Initially they were not interested in fully integrating with the rest of the campus.

A VIEW OF JERUSALEM, WITH A SERIES OF OUTDOOR ROOMS ANCHORED BY A TOWER

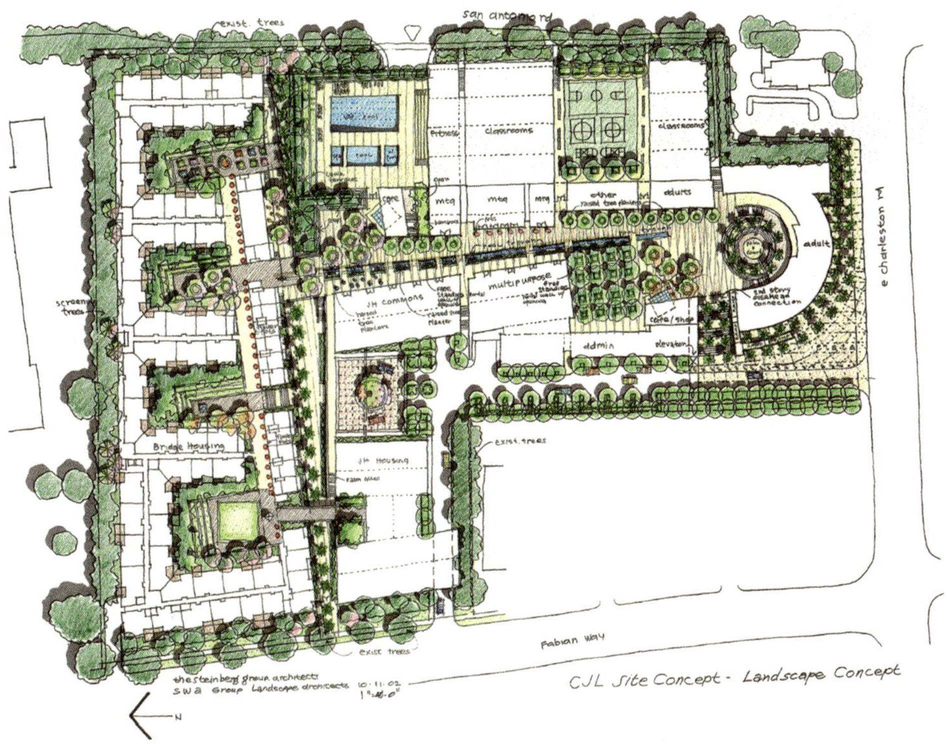

RIGHT THE INITIAL PLAN, WITH BUILDINGS DEFINING THE OUTDOOR ROOMS.

I presented my first overall big picture: I imagined our own Jerusalem, a village of different communities each with their distinct identities, enriched by being able to share resources. I wanted walkways that would wander amid a jumble of bustling life. I envisioned a living mosaic, where many different lives and stories would thrive together. Common areas would include a community park, fitness center, preschool, meeting rooms, and a cultural hall.

THE BEACON

Beyond fulfilling the various needs of the constituents, I wanted the Campus for Jewish Life to include an identifiable presence in the larger region as a symbol of how it would be contributing to the whole of Silicon Valley life.

My first concept sketch highlighted an iconic tower, facing east toward Jerusalem. As the tallest element on the site and an anchor of the Town Square, the Tower would be visible from blocks away. Like the French cathedrals, our beacon would proclaim our community's confidence in the future.

AN IMPASSE; AND THEN A MIRACLE

At this moment, the Jewish Senior Living Group discovered that they had hit a wall: the financial

BELOW LEFT THE WALK STREET OR *MIDRAHOV*, PROVIDES THE JOURNEY.

BELOW RIGHT THE TOWN SQUARE, ANCHORED BY THE LIGHT TOWER.

model for assisted living was no longer a viable option to support its share of debt service.

Following advice from its financial consultants, the group proposed shifting the project from a stand-alone, assisted-living facility to a Continuing Care Retirement Community (CCRC) model that included independent living, assisted living, and memory-support facilities, financed by the residents themselves, who would buy into the community. With this paradigm shift, the 80,000-square-foot facility would need to became a 240,000-square-foot CCRC with 193 apartments. Triple the original size, the senior living program now dwarfed the JCC. Unfortunately, the campus simply did not have sufficient room for both while retaining the originally anticipated open space desired.

Bridge also brought a new challenge to the table. The city was requiring greater-than-anticipated setbacks along the property line shared with an adjacent, industrial neighbor, reducing the number of units and square footage permitted. To balance the financial requirements and now-reduced mass, Bridge decided to sell three of its four acres to Sares Regis, a residential developer, who would construct market-rate flats and townhomes. Sares would require easy access to parking and shared access to the community park, which would include a soccer field. Bridge retained one acre on which to develop low-income, affordable senior housing, and they would require easy access to public transport and very low construction costs.

Previous parameters flew out the window. My initial vision was now obsolete. The honeymoon was officially over.

Early in my career I learned never to present a client with an option that I didn't want to pursue because the client might become fixed on it and never let go. But in this case, I was in a bind: the inviting, open spaces I envisioned for the campus would be consumed with the now-oversized senior living project, while the campus anchor — the JCC — was becoming dwarfed.

On our second attempt to devise an acceptable master plan, all the constituents gathered around a huge model. With great discomfort, I presented a plan that I could not embrace, attempting to force the additional 160,000 square feet onto the site. Besides the significant reductions in quality and outdoor space, the site dimensions would force us to move the community park to the middle of the site, pushing the constituencies away from one another. My hope for a single mosaic woven together into a coherent community was in jeopardy.

The stakeholders actually agreed with me that the sprawling solution was not ideal, but

BELOW THE MODEL, DOMINATED BY THE VAST SENIOR HOUSING AREAS, ON THE RIGHT IN BEIGE.

BOTTOM THE ALTERNATIVES FOR THE MIX OF FOR-PROFIT AND NOT-FOR-PROFIT HOUSING. THE THIRD, WITH THE PREMIUM POSITION GIVEN TO THE NOT-FOR-PROFIT, BECAME FINAL.

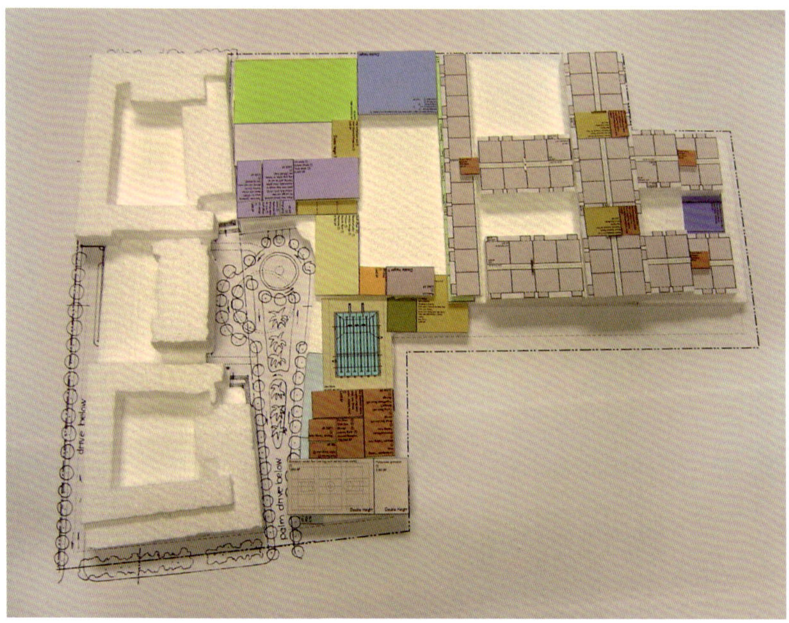

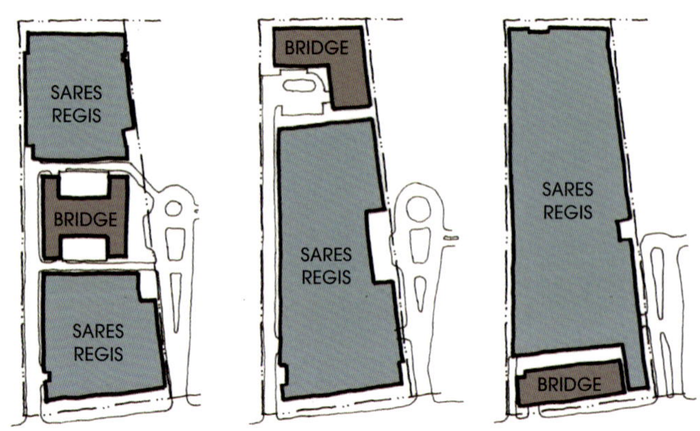

the cold, hard, economic facts of the matter required it.

After exhaustive studies, it became clear that there were a very limited number of options to shuffle four large users on a fixed piece of land.

But then an idea occurred to me, a radical and disruptive concept that might just give each of the stakeholders what they needed. I realized that if I was allowed to move the senior residences *above* the JCC's space, I would be able to return the open space to the main campus and allow all of the communities to integrate once again.

While this design solution would unlock the land-use challenge, it would create a multitude of long-term ownership issues: a shotgun marriage to which the JCC and Jewish Senior Living Group would have to commit by agreeing to occupy shared, rather than independent buildings. Previously unrelated organizations would become inextricably tied to heating, cooling, security, and maintenance for the life of the campus, which would extend beyond the life of any of us currently at the table.

This time I presented my solution, hoping the benefits would outweigh the increased practicalities for all stakeholders. They did, and my proposal was unanimously accepted.

FRIED CHICKEN

Buoyed by this success, I took the opportunity to raise another prickly, unresolved issue.

Early in the land-acquisition process, the group tried to purchase an additional, small, but strategically significant parcel that removed a major corner of the campus. The parcel was owned and occupied by Kentucky Fried Chicken.

Every time I visited the site, I was assaulted by the whiff of fried chicken. I feared it would taint campus visitors' experience and diminish membership. So I complained, asking if we really wanted to plan a community whose street identity would forever be a KFC?

The project director summoned me to her office the following day. "Isn't it about time for you to do your job rather than continuing to introduce upsetting roadblocks?"

Still, I persisted. Eventually, the group agreed to go back and try once more with KFC. After more delays, incredible efforts, and negotiation aided by an additional donor, the community purchased the signature corner, which I was now able to incorporate into my planning.

AGREEMENT ON PROCESS

Frustrated by the many conflicting opinions that were endlessly dropped on my plate, I tried to replace the often subjective and piecemeal process with some kind of organized objectivity. I introduced nine design principles that could offer a neutral measuring stick by which to evaluate proposed design solutions through a common lens. My strategy was to obtain buy-in to the fundamental design concepts so that I might be able to create a new solution.

THE KENTUCKY FRIED CHICKEN CORNER

Seven principles were adopted, and eventually guided the design. It would take several years to reach consensus.

THE 7 DESIGN PRINCIPLES

1. COMMUNITY

Three strategic solutions would fundamentally shape the community.

The Cultural Hall, the most visible space, and shared with the broader surrounding Palo Alto community, would anchor the main corner previously occupied by KFC.

The narrow leg off a quieter street provided an ideal entry drive, perfect for the comings and goings of members utilizing the Fitness Center, who did not need to delve deep into the site. The large entry drive could accommodate traffic surges, drop-offs, and pick-ups, access to the JCC garage, and access to a second, separate garage for Bridge Housing and Sares Regis residents.

The final piece of the puzzle was to shape the bulk and mass of the 240,000-square-foot senior residences, now a much more expansive model featuring eight units per floor. I envisioned each building as an oversized home. The glazed bridges that linked them would serve as interior porches. Such shared amenities would foster connection between the two linked houses and offer a route connecting all eight houses together. The bridges and balconies also offered close visual observation of the buzzing campus below without requiring the seniors to actually physically engage with the activity if they preferred not to.

The adjacent, four-acre residential parcel, home to both low-income seniors and market-rate families, was designed in conjunction with the campus for easy mingling among

THE 12-ACRE FINAL MASTER PLAN.

RIGHT MODEL SHOWING THE CONCEPT OF *ALIYAH*, OR "GOING-UP" INTO THE COMMUNITY.

FAR RIGHT MODEL OF THE TOWER, AT A HEIGHT THAT MAKES IT VISIBLE TO THE SURROUNDING COMMUNITY.

all populations. Through its diverse mix, the campus would invite the broader community to participate in extensive educational, social, wellness, cultural, and recreational opportunities.

2. SECURITY

Jewish institutions of all kinds are targets for violent attacks. With that in mind, some of the earliest design thoughts about a 12-acre Jewish campus also raised the specter of ending up with a walled city. This would have isolated the campus from the rest of the community, and would have been a terrible result.

Fortunately, the site confronted two significant environmental challenges: it was situated in a low-lying, floodplain area, and, as a mixed blessing, it was threatened by a contaminated groundwater plume originating on an industrial site upstream, making its way beneath our site to San Francisco Bay. To address the floodplain situation, the building code required new construction be built no less than three feet above the existing grade. Addressing the toxic plume presented far more cumbersome measures.

Initially, the Regional Quality Water Control Board prohibited any excavation for underground parking. Officials were especially concerned about the toxic threat to children and seniors who would inhabit the new structures. After months of studies that delayed the project, the water board imposed additional mitigation measures that would add millions of dollars to the project: overall site excavation to install an industrial-grade, waterproof membrane below the building's foundations, and an additional level of waterproofing to individually seal each building's first-floor concrete slab.

This came as shocking and crippling news to the campus's future occupants, nearly threatening to derail the project. I asked them to give me time to think through alternatives. Not able to excavate and required to be at least three feet above the ground, it made sense to me to elevate further, creating an entire level of parking at ground level, between the plume and a "podium" on which the entire campus would rest.

Raising the entire campus on a podium also achieved a natural security. Instead of a walled city, the campus could be a higher city, with a feeling of openness, yet with controllable access. And the most protected area of the campus, far

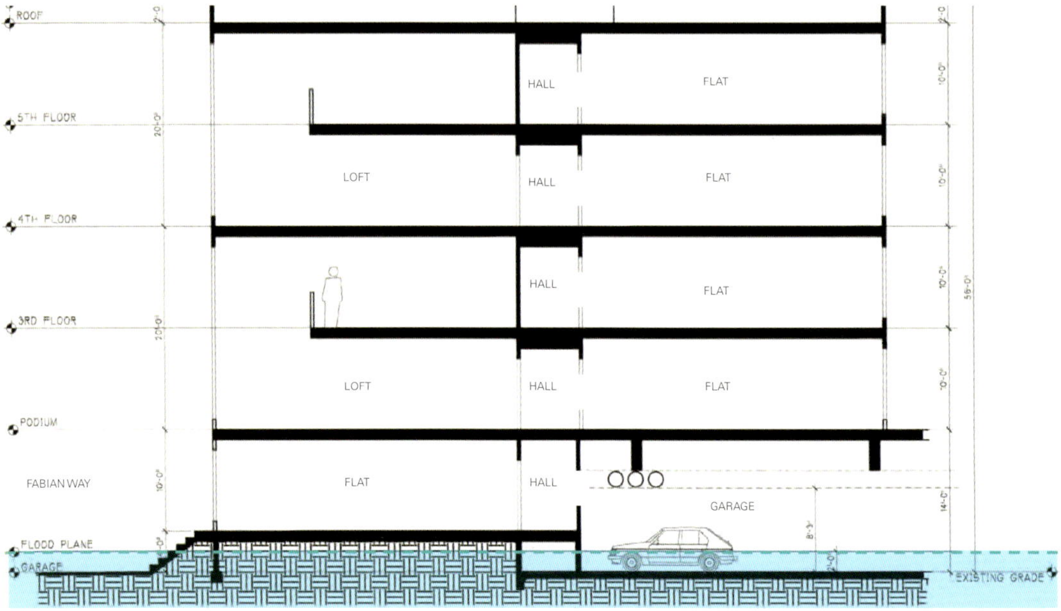

LEFT SECTION THROUGH THE HOUSING. THE CONTAMINATED WATER FORCED EVERYTHING HIGHER, BEGINNING WITH THE PARKING GARAGE, NOW AT GRADE LEVEL, WITH THE NEW PODIUM 15 FEET ABOVE.

BELOW SITE SECTION.

from vehicular and pedestrian access, would be the preschool.

With an understanding of the compromise, all parties embraced this solution.

3. ALIYAH

The elevation of the entire campus offered us flexible traffic patterns distributed to all three adjacent streets, which was good. But it also brought new challenges: how to connect the elevated podium level with the street 15 feet below? And how to minimize the daunting perception from the street of the looming new podium level? We wanted to create a campus that was integrated with the existing area and was mindful of the pedestrian experience.

A concept from my Jewish background provided just the right storyline. The Hebrew word *Aliyah* means "ascent," or "going up." It implies the conscious effort to move from the mundane to the sacred, from the ordinary to a higher place. When a diaspora Jew moves to Israel, he is said to be making *Aliyah*, or ascending to Jerusalem.

In our case, the very act of engaging with the Jewish community through the JCC and Jewish senior residences — entailing graceful transitions from the street-level, public arena to the podium-level, Jewish community campus — represented an act of *Aliyah*. A ground-floor lobby serving the senior residences extended a welcoming portal from the busy, Palo Alto artery up to one of the eight senior houses. Wide staircases with extended landings invited campus visitors to bring their best, elevated selves to the community found at the podium level.

The design of the Campus for Jewish Life converted vertical transitions from obstacles into

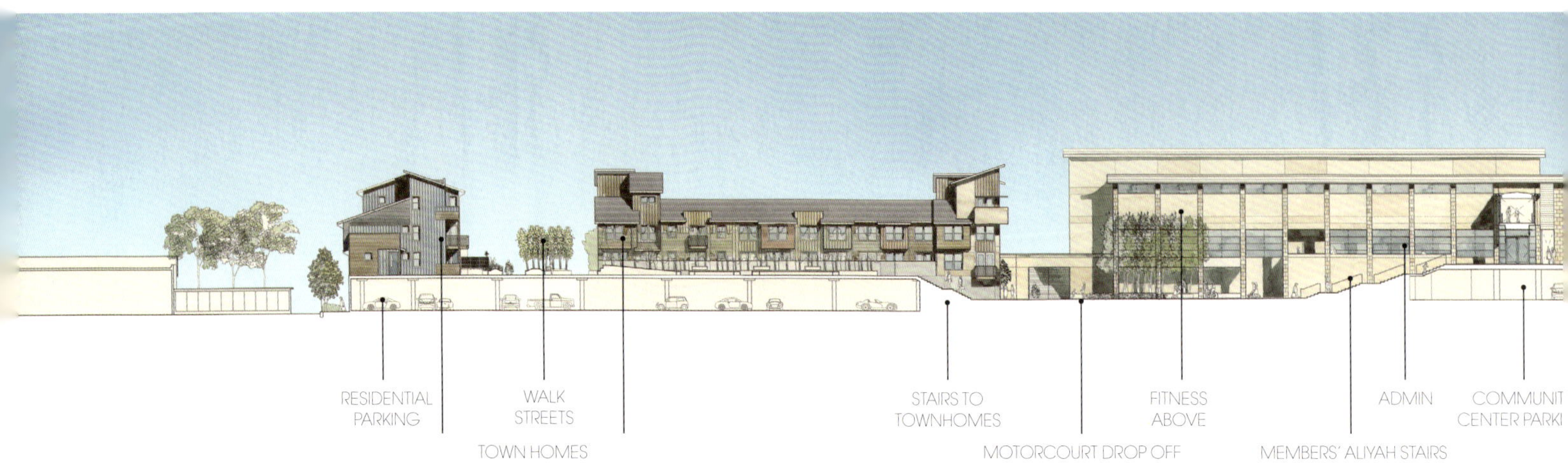

opportunities for the celebration of community as a spiritually uplifting endeavor, literally raising ourselves up.

4. THE OUTDOORS: JOURNEYS AND ROOMS

Jerusalem

The story of *Aliyah*, of ascent to Jerusalem, became a guiding narrative for me. I imagined a community campus based on the Old City, with varied, unfolding outdoor rooms and buildings of Jerusalem stone. I envisioned spontaneous interactions that would be as important as the more organized gatherings of people, and designed circuitous pedestrian walk streets that revealed outdoor courtyards, with wayfinding through the use of environmental cues: portals that led from one space to another, building façades that telegraphed their activities within, and, from many locations, the steady presence of the Tower that would help the skyline make sense whenever one might catch a glimpse of it.

Serial Visioning

Like nudging a friend who is nodding off, serial visioning is characterized by gentle deviations in alignment and quite small variations in projections and setbacks. In the campus, the focus is on the experience of the pedestrian with a narrative created by a variety of sense experiences. A narrow street, leading to what feels like an open space ahead. The experience of a moment of tranquility in the open space, and then moving on to the next part of the journey. Together, these deviations have a disproportionately powerful effect in the third dimension. A 7.5-degree variation in plan originating from adjacent streets eventually develops into a full palette of variations in shaping the size and character of outdoor rooms.

Town Square

My vision was not a singular experience but one of multiple, intersecting circulation routes and a pedestrian-friendly collection of outdoor, communal rooms of varying dimensions and character, all woven together. The largest of the outdoor rooms, the Town Square, has become the crossroads of all activities, linking paths to preschool, fitness, administration, the café, and the community park. It is the community living room, accommodating celebrations, concerts, and ceremonies.

Midrahov

The streets of Jerusalem are closed to traffic from the Sabbath until Sunday morning. The *Midrahov*, or walk street, was a nod to Jerusalem's Ben Yehuda Street, alive with activity on Saturday nights, when crowds pour into the street to mill around the thoroughfare, enjoying cafés, shops, and socialization. On our campus, our *Midrahov* was laid out with a forced perspective exaggerating the dynamics of the "street," interrupted by entrances to preschool, the teen lounge, adult program spaces, and senior activity centers.

5. HOW THE BUILDINGS TELL

I wanted each building to reflect its unique purpose and function, and the collection of buildings to reflect a unified whole. I used an exposed steel frame and a taut surface over it to evoke the human body being exercised in the Fitness Center. The interior accent color is red, evoking the blood pumping through bodies in motion. The preschool is distinct with a panel system with exposed fasteners, conveying work in progress — a place where *building character* in our children is taking place. Senior residences

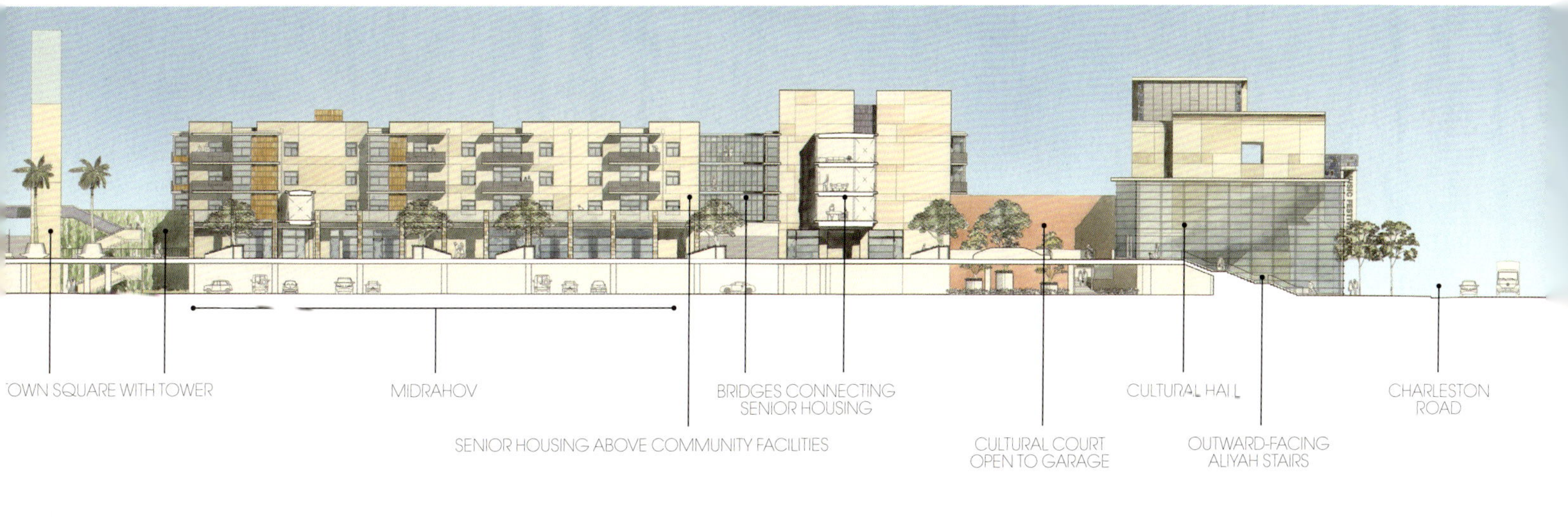

THE BUILDINGS SHAPE A VARIETY OF OUTDOOR ROOMS.

OVERLEAF THE PRIMARY STREETSCAPE OF THE CAMPUS.

are clad in shingles to celebrate some of the weathering that comes with earned wisdom. Paralleling a community made up of unique individuals who combine to create a powerful collective, the Cultural Hall utilizes glazed tiles of varying colors and patterns to create a cohesive mosaic façade.

6. THE HARVEST PROVIDES A COLOR PALETTE

Deuteronomy 8:8 describes the Land of Israel as a "land of wheat and barley, of (grape) vines, figs, and pomegranates, and of olives for oil and (date) honey." Those offerings of the first fruits — brought to the Temple in Jerusalem on the Jewish holiday of *Shavuot* — became the palette for both exterior and interior color schemes. One of the fruits' colors accents each of the eight senior residence buildings, with interior carpeting and wall accents containing bits of each.

7. JEWISH SYMBOLISM OR A UNIVERSAL ARCHITECTURAL LANGUAGE?

One of the early design decisions involved the degree to which religious symbols should be part of the architecture. With strong convictions on both sides of the issue, we were unable to reach consensus. The campus would not showcase overt Jewish symbols and motifs, but I still wanted to create an authentic *Jewish* place. The elements would add to the experience of those who recognized them as references to Judaism but would not be required to appreciate the design. For example, Judaism teaches us to look upward to God for inspiration, so the fitness, cultural, and administration buildings include the recurring motif of a roof that ends in a delicate upward curve, just giving a hint toward the infinite.

APPROVAL

Seven years after I got the commission, the Palo Alto City Council voted for approval. Imagine my overwhelming joy when the *Palo Alto Weekly* — the local newspaper of record — reported the council's unanimous approval of "the largest, most complex project ever built in Palo Alto."

BELOW LEFT TO RIGHT PRESCHOOL CLADDING OF PANELIZED SYSTEM WITH EXPOSED FASTENERS CONVEYS THAT EDUCATION IS A WORK IN PROGRESS.

THE SENIOR RESIDENT SHINGLE CLADDING CELEBRATES EARNED WISDOM.

THE CULTURAL HALL TILING IS A MOSAIC, REFLECTING THE DIVERSITY OF THE COMMUNITY.

OPPOSITE ABOVE THE PILLARS ARE CLAD IN JERUSALEM STONE. THE FITNESS CENTER SHOWS OFF ITS STRUCTURE OF SKIN STRETCHED OVER BONE.

OPPOSITE BELOW LEFT FACING THE FITNESS CENTER; ACROSS THE ENTRY DRIVE, SARES REGIS DWELLINGS.

OPPOSITE BELOW RIGHT THE TOWNHOUSE WALK STREETS CONNECT TO THE PLAY FIELD.

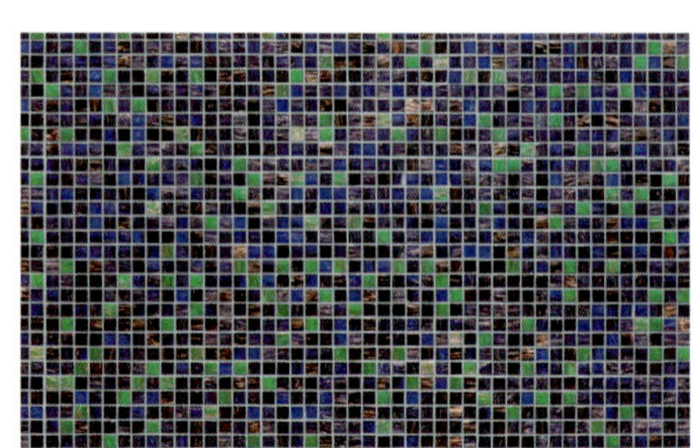

THE INDOOR WARM-WATER POOL SERVES BOTH THE PRESCHOOLERS WITH A SLOPING ENTRY APRON, WHILE SENIORS CAN ENJOY THEIR EASILY ENCLOSED THERAPY AREA (FAR TOP).

RIGHT THE OUTDOOR POOL, WITH ITS STRUCTURE FOR CANVAS SHADES, LEFT. THE INDOOR POOL IS BEHIND THE GLASS AT THE EDGE OF THE DECK.

BELOW LEFT TREADMILLS OVERLOOK THE SPORT FIELD SO EXERCISING PARENTS CAN WATCH THEIR CHILDREN DOING THE SAME. RED ACCENTS THROUGHOUT CONNECT WITH NOTIONS OF CIRCULATING BLOOD.

BELOW RIGHT RECLINING WORKOUTS GET A LOWER CEILING AND SOFTENED WESTERN LIGHT.

OPPOSITE THE MEMBERS' *ALIYAH* (GOING-UP), PASSING UNDER A BRIDGE WITH EXERCISERS WITHIN, AND ENTERING THE TOWN SQUARE BEYOND.

RIGHT THE TOWN SQUARE. THE MAMMOTH PALM POTS CREATE SMALL GATHERING SPACES.

ABOVE THE TOWN SQUARE CROSSROADS, SERVED BY A CAFÉ, BELOW LEFT.

LEFT ANOTHER VIEW OF THE TOWN SQUARE, FROM THE TERRACED AMPHITHEATER.

OPPOSITE BELOW THE TERRACE ON THE UPPER LEFT RESERVES THE MOST PRIVILEGED VANTAGE POINT FOR MEMORY-IMPAIRED SENIORS.

OVERLEAF THE *MIDRAHOV*, BRINGING TOGETHER A STREET LIFE OF FAMILIES, PRESCHOOLERS, AND THE TEEN CENTER IN THE MIDDLE.

BELOW THE PRESCHOOL IS PLACED TO CATCH THE WARMING MORNING LIGHT. THE AWNINGS FILTER THE VIEW FROM THE SENIORS ABOVE, AND VICE VERSA.

RIGHT SOME SENIORS START THEIR DAY WITH COFFEE ON THEIR TERRACES, WATCHING THE CHILDREN GATHER.

תאנה
זית
גפן

ABOVE THE *MIDRAHOV* NARROWS AT THE FAR END, INCREASING THE ENERGY.

LEFT SUN SHADES, PLAYING OFF THE JERUSALEM STONE ARCADE, MIRROR THE UPWARD CURVES FOUND IN THE ROOFS.

OPPOSITE BELOW FOR SENIORS, A QUIET PERCH FOR OBSERVING THE *MIDRAHOV* WITHOUT THE REQUIREMENT OF FULL ENGAGEMENT.

BELOW FROM INSIDE THE TEEN CENTER, AT THE HEART OF THE COMMUNITY, AND THE OPPOSITE OF ISOLATED.

RIGHT A RUST STEEL SCULPTURE OF 12 COLUMNS (FOR THE 12 TRIBES OF ISRAEL) DEFINES A GATHERING AREA AT THE CULTURAL CENTER, NEAR THE END OF THE *MIDRAHOV*.

FAR LEFT THE PARK-LIKE GARDENS OF ONE OF THE SENIOR COURTYARDS.

LEFT THE LOBBY IS A SUN-FILLED INDOOR PORCH THAT OVERLOOKS ALL THE COMINGS AND GOINGS OF THE CAMPUS.

BELOW CHILDREN VISITING THE OTHER SENIOR COURTYARD. THE SENIOR DINING ROOM BORDERS THE FAR END.

BELOW THE CULTURAL HALL COURTYARD, A FAVORITE FOR WEDDING CELEBRATIONS, OVERLOOKED BY SENIOR RESIDENTS ON THEIR BALCONIES.

RIGHT THE CULTURAL HALL INTERIOR. THE UPHOLSTERED SEATS CAN BE PUSHED AWAY TO CREATE A DINING AND DANCING ROOM, ON A FLOOR REMINISCENT OF THE TENTS OF NOMADIC FOREBEARS FROM MILLENNIA PAST, WITH THE TENT MOTIF REINFORCED BY THE POLES ALONG THE FAR WALL. ALL CONCERTS ARE RECORDED AND AVAILABLE FOR RESIDENTS IN THEIR HOMES OR EVEN DURING EXERCISE.

TEN YEARS LATER: AN UNEXPECTED COMMUNITY

At the tenth-anniversary celebration, I found myself sitting with the original project manager who had reprimanded me to stop raising challenges and "do my job" all those years ago. We were surrounded by hundreds of people milling about the Town Square, and hundreds more enjoying a carnival on the verdant new community park. As we soaked in the moment, we wondered to one another how the campus was measuring up to the original vision, and what has unfolded beyond what we imagined?

During the design phase, we found ourselves trying to balance divisions within the greater Bay Area Jewish community. The large Israeli ex-pat community — drawn both by Stanford University and the rich, high-technology sector — operated quite apart from the American Jewish community, with its own social, educational, and recreational programs. Better integration with Israelis had been a goal, but it seemed a very high hurdle to surmount as their identity was national, not religious or cultural.

However, today, through the tremendous efforts and creativity of professional and volunteer leaders, the Campus for Jewish Life is home to an ongoing, active, and vibrant Israeli community, hosting a Hebrew school, Hebrew-language lectures and classes, holiday celebrations, and more.

Another division concerned the balance between the observant, religious community and more liberal, secular members. During the planning stages, the level of religious observance on the campus was a hot-button issue. While some expressed outrage that the café on the Town Square be anything but kosher, others proclaimed the café would be kosher over their dead bodies. It seemed an intractable situation in which we were certain to alienate one group or the other. Also, some suggested the campus include a synagogue, as some other JCCs did. In the end, the café was not kosher, though vegetarian options were available, and no synagogue was located on the campus.

Yet, ten years later, there are two very observant groups happily occupying their campus quarters. Lining the entry drive into the campus is a strip of office space identified as "Future Use," which we imagined might someday provide satellite office space for affiliated Jewish agencies. Today, that space is occupied by the Jewish Study Network (JSN),

A CLASSROOM FOR THE JEWISH STUDY NETWORK ADDS TO THE FULL SPECTRUM OF CAMPUS LIFE.

JEWISH GIRLS IN OBSERVANT DRESS ON THE BASKETBALL COURT.

devoted to raising the level of Jewish literacy in the Bay Area. JSN employs a group of observant young rabbis, traditional in their practice and schooled to teach traditional explanations of Jewish law, recognizable for their dark suits, white dress shirts, and head coverings — even on the warmest Palo Alto days.

Additionally, Meira Academy, a private Orthodox Jewish high school for girls, provides a full Jewish day-school curriculum alongside a demanding general studies program. Late in the afternoon, it is not unusual to see Meira girls in their opaque tights, pleated navy skirts, and striped Oxford cloth shirts running up and down the basketball court. Although the Orthodox were not a part of the original vision, their presence has enriched the campus and the community.

A MODEL FOR THE FUTURE?

The Campus for Jewish Life offers city planners an innovative template for adapting to accommodate the inevitable population increase and critical transportation needs of the future, while retaining a vital sense of community that people will want to be a part of. The variety of uses and users make the campus a valuable model for future architecture and planners as they wrap their arms around understanding and embracing density. As under-optimized sites throughout the valley are tapped for residential use in the coming decades, Silicon Valley will have to devise new ways to add housing for hundreds of thousands of new residents — without sacrificing the Bay region's exceptional quality of life. The Campus for Jewish Life is a prime experiment in testing possible solutions.

AN UNSEEN BEACON

The Jewish "day" begins at dusk, when natural daylight recedes. Like time, light, too, is a fundamental concept in Judaism. Whether through *Shabbat* candles, holiday candles, or *yahrzeit* candles lit on the anniversary of the death of a loved one, light conveys holiness. In the Creation story in the Book of Genesis, God said, "Let there be light!" and God saw the light and deemed it "good." In another reference, the people of Israel are commanded to be "a light unto the nations," or an example of how to live a good life.

Combining the ideas of time and light, my design for the campus Tower perceives Jewish time and events in a "carillon of light." Its most significant presence would be at the beginning of the Jewish day (dusk) when it would display a pattern of lights incorporating color, intensity, frequency, and pattern, perhaps increasing color and intensity on Fridays as *Shabbat* approaches. *Rosh chodesh* — the new month — could also be reflected with color and patterns appropriate to the season.

Unfortunately, budget constraints have indefinitely postponed the completion of the Light Tower. Without it, the Campus for Jewish Life is a little bit less of a beacon to the larger community and a little bit less of an inspiration to its immediate family than it might be. In an often-darkening world, the Tower remains a bell unrung, a voice not yet heard, a light not yet kindled.

THE TOWER AS IT WOULD HAVE BEEN SEEN UPON ENTERING THE TOWN SQUARE.

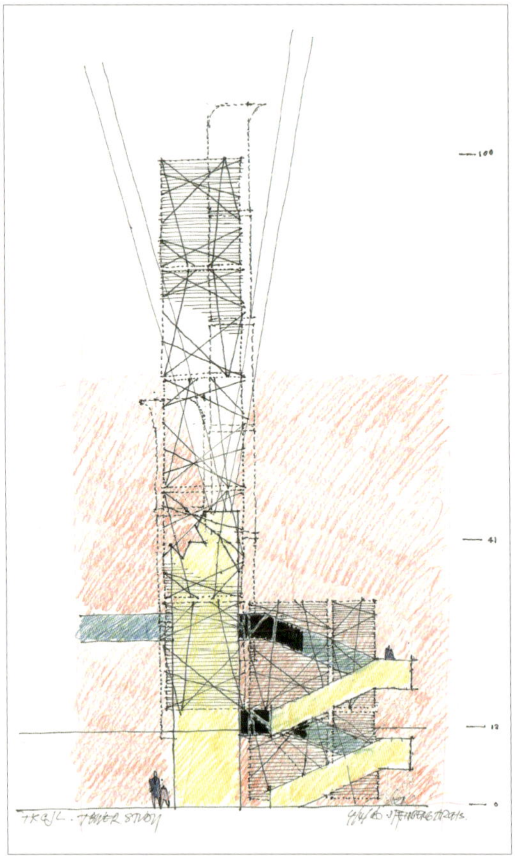

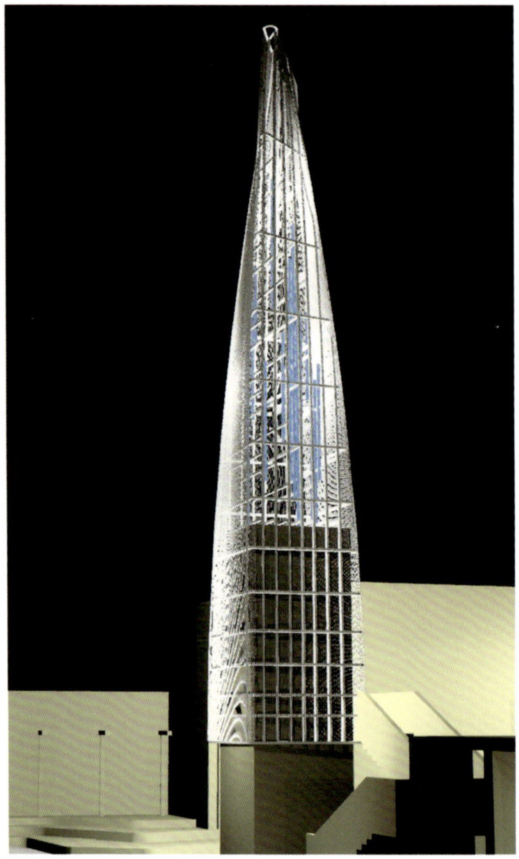

FAR LEFT CONCEPTUAL SKETCH OF THE LOWER AND UPPER COMPONENTS OF THE TOWER, AS PER THE CITY OF PALO ALTO GUIDELINES: "THE SCULPTURAL TOWER SHALL NOT EXCEED A FOOTPRINT OF 12' × 12', SHALL HAVE A LOWER SOLID PORTION NOT TO EXCEED 65' ABOVE GRADE, AND A SCULPTURAL DESIGN ABOVE THE SOLID PORTION NOT TO EXCEED 96 FEET ABOVE GRADE. THE SCULPTURAL TOWER DESIGN SHALL NOT INCLUDE BRIGHT-LIGHT ELEMENTS AS A PRIMARY DESIGN ELEMENT. LOW-LEVEL ACCENT LIGHTING, IF INCLUDED AS PART OF THE DESIGN, SHALL BE THE LOWEST LEVEL POSSIBLE TO ACHIEVE THE DESIRED EFFECT."

LEFT THE SOLID PART, BUILT IN PHASE 1, CONTAINS AN ELEVATOR. THE UPPER PART OF THE LIGHT TOWER, NOT YET BUILT, IS A LATTICE OF METAL AND FLEXIBLE LIGHTING SYSTEMS.

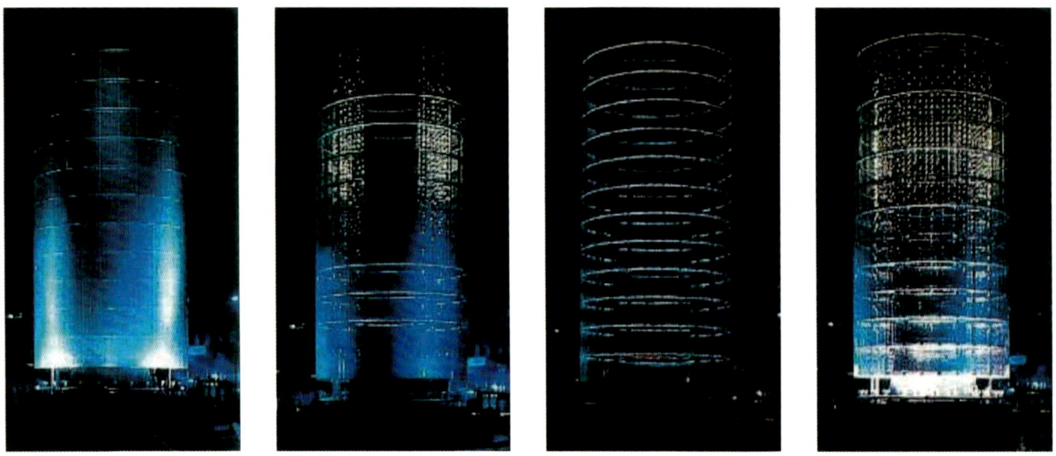

FROM LEFT LIGHTING STRATEGIES: OPAQUE, EXTERIOR WASH, SKELETAL, AND INTERIOR WASH.

OPPOSITE THE BASE IS ORIENTED TO THE PALO ALTO GRID. AS THE TOWER INCREASES IN ALTITUDE, IN A MANNER SIMILAR TO JEWS AT PRAYER, IT ALSO TURNS TO FACE JERUSALEM.

1 ARCHITECTURE IS THE PURSUIT OF PERFECTION
2 ARCHITECTURE IS INHERENTLY DIS-RUPTIVE
3 ARCHITECTURE BUILDS COMMUNITY
4 ARCHITECTURE EXISTS IN TENSION WITH NATURE
5 Architecture is Storytelling
6 ARCHITECTURE TELLS US HOW TO USE IT
7 ARCHITECTURE IS ART
8 ARCHITECTURE REQUIRES LEADERSHIP
9 ARCHITECTURE IS INNOVATION

Architecture strives to be the perfect embodiment of an idea as free as possible from all flaws or defects. It requires a process of methodical and relentless refinement.

Architecture doesn't exist in isolation. It is, in effect, like joining an existing conversation. Architecture should be responsive to its context, purpose, and moment in time.

Architecture is a social art that choreographs human interacti(-_-)n.

ARCHITECTURE STRIVES TO CO-EXIST WITH NATURE'S FORCES INCLUDING GRAVITY, WATER, AND LIGHT.

At its best, architecture originates from a single organizing narrative, and every supporting element is an expression of that same force.

A building's function, hierarchy, and navigation should support an intuitive understanding.

Architecture goes beyond the utilitarian skill of responding to physical and functional requirements. Elevating the spirit through rebellious exploration, it provides new perspectives on the known, allowing others to see things differently.

Architecture requires leadership that can develop a clear vision, build consensus, and sustain that vision over time.

ARCHITECTURE BRINGS IDEAS, CREATIVE THOUGHT, OR IMAGINATION TO ADDRESS EXISTING CONDITIONS, NEW REQUIREMENTS, OR UNARTICULATED NEEDS, RESULTING IN PROGRESS FOR HUMANITY.

在路上
试水中国
ON THE ROAD
THE CHINA TEST

In the summer of 2003, our architecture firm was flying high. We were hard at work on the design of the San Jose International Airport, the gateway to the world-renowned Silicon Valley; we had received the commission of a lifetime to design a 12-acre, Jewish community campus in Palo Alto; and the firm had expanded into Southern California.

My father, Goody, had retired, and now, at age 52, I was President of The Steinberg Group. I loved spending time in the company of my parents, and I adored my beautiful family — my wife Alice, and our three wonderful children Jacob, Talia, and Rachel, a college senior, a college freshman, and a high-school freshman, nicknamed strawberry, chocolate, and vanilla, respectively, for their red, brunette, and blonde hair. The kids were thriving. Life was good.

July 23, 2003, was a beautiful day in the San Francisco Bay Area. I was enjoying a scenic drive to St. Helena, in the Northern California wine country, where the firm was holding an off-site retreat to thank the team for bringing the firm such success. Staying at the location selected would be a perk: St. Helena's Harvest Inn, which I had recently renovated for my friend, hotelier Rick Swig, whose family is well-known for founding the Fairmont Hotels. I was looking forward to strolling in the redwoods, relaxing poolside, and savoring a good Napa Cab.

And then a phone call interrupted my reverie.

It was my brother, Tom, calling from New York.

"Where are you?" he asked.

"On my way to St. Helena."

"I want you to pull over." The line was quiet as I identified a safe spot to pull off the highway, crowded with tourists making their way from vineyard to vineyard.

"OK," I said. "What's up?"

"Rob," he said, "Jacob is dead."

In the instant that Tom's words left his mouth, the world as I knew it came crashing down so violently it accosted all of my senses. As Alice, who is one of the most astute, intuitive observers of life, told our daughters that day, "Stop what you are doing. Look around you. Remember this moment, because life as we know it will never be the same."

Jacob was a little red-haired kid with boundless energy. Every morning he awoke with zeal and asked the same question, "What are we going to do today?" Only the finite number of hours in the day limited his ability to dream up and execute each next idea.

At Occidental College, Jake was elected president of his freshman class. He traveled the nation singing with the Glee Club, deejayed a campus radio show, edited the arts and entertainment section of the school newspaper, and served as a college ambassador, speaking at parent and alumni events. He talked his way into being a "seat filler" at the Academy Awards, temporarily slipping into the seats of celebrity presenters so that televised audience shots would show a full house. After the broadcast, he snuck into some of the Oscar after-parties and mingled with the movie stars. His dream was to be a Hollywood producer, so the summer internship he had landed with a nationally renowned talent agency in New York City was a dream come true.

But unbeknownst to us, while in New York, Jacob began taking medication prescribed by a doctor in California, which triggered a chemical imbalance in the brain. As his work colleagues told us, he

OPPOSITE THE AUTHOR AND HIS SON, JACOB.

BELOW FROM LEFT, RACHEL, JACOB, AND TALIA, AKA VANILLA, STRAWBERRY AND CHOCOLATE.

seemed to experience a manic episode. When uncharacteristic and erratic behavior prompted his supervisor to ask him to go home for the day, he adamantly refused. And when security was called to escort him out, he broke away from the guard, hurled a large chair through the 24th-story midtown Manhattan window, and leaped out after it. In an instant, life was extinguished.

In Jake's apartment, Alice and I found his empty prescription bottles. The medical examiner confirmed the medication was in Jacob's system, at prescribed dosage levels. He had not overdosed. Yet something had gone terribly wrong.

My anguish was so overwhelming it literally crippled me. I couldn't work, couldn't focus, couldn't function. Much of the next few years is a fog that even today is only partially retraceable.

The Great Leap Forward

It took years of anguish and struggle for me to emerge from my grief enough to carry on some semblance of life. When I did, I felt a strong need for a shift in direction. I was fortunate to have the encouragement of colleagues within and outside the firm to point me toward my next pursuit.

In 2004, my close friend and colleague, David Nieh, was recruited from the San Jose Redevelopment Agency to establish the Shanghai offices of a prominent international architecture firm. Whenever we spoke by phone, he was effervescent about the extensive development taking place in Shanghai and all over China.

"You wouldn't believe what's happening here," he told me. "It's crazy. You've got to come see for yourself. I've never seen anything like it."

There was encouragement to expand into China from inside the firm as well. Two colleagues — Henry Zeng and Hong Chen — saw the explosive development occurring in China as a huge potential opportunity for us. Being of Chinese descent and eager to contribute to advancing our firm, they urged me to consider seeking work in this nascent overseas market.

Over and over again I demurred. But finally, at the urging of David, Henry, and Hong, in 2007, Henry and I made our first exploratory visit to China.

The Chinese economy was vast, with real-estate development a key driver. Developers competed fiercely to differentiate their projects, and one important distinction was the cachet of a foreign architect, especially an architect from the United States. There were many barriers to entry, not least of which was the chaotic, often impenetrable business environment, but I could see the abundant creative and financial opportunity if I could muster the wherewithal to take on the challenge.

I needed a "reset" to draw myself out of the pain and paralysis of losing Jacob. In the decision to explore opportunities in China, I found the fresh focus that could propel me back into the world of the living.

Henry and Hong relocated to Shanghai from San Jose, and the first eight years that we did business in China, I traveled there every six weeks or so for a stay of at least a week.

I had been counseled on more than one occasion that the stature of our first client would greatly affect our future. In China, architects are classed not only on the quality of their work, but also on the reputation and perception of their clients in the marketplace. With that in mind, we had to be highly selective about our first commission. The initial projects would set our status for decades to come.

In the nine months of our aggressive marketing initiative, I made the 14-hour flight to China every six weeks, visiting each of three cities — Hong Kong, Shanghai, and Beijing — and made two to three presentations a day for seven to ten days in pursuit of the right client. As one year became two, the pressure on us to deliver simply grew. Colleagues suggested we give it up. Members of the firm were grumbling about the endless cost. And I was exhausting myself trying to run our three California offices from China.

Henry, my partner, had been trying for many months to reconnect with his old friend, Mr. Chen, from their early days as young architects in China. Mr. Chen had gone on to become a powerful senior executive in Overseas Chinese Town (OCT), one of the mammoth government-owned development companies.

We finally received an invitation to meet Mr. Chen. Henry was quite deferential around him, even though they had once been peers. Mr. Chen spoke so softly you had to lean in to hear him. He had a Zen calmness about him. One could read his status by the way he was surrounded: others took notes for him, paid his tabs, chauffeured him wherever he wanted to go. He was both a powerful business figure and seemed to be a power in the Party. You just sensed it.

Mr. Chen invited us to play golf with him. Each of us was given three caddies to follow us around, protecting us from the mild sun with little umbrellas. Every shot was greeted with their applause, followed by fresh cool towels. After one tee shot, as I was strolling along the edge of the fairway, I was suddenly stung in the butt by something shocking. I spun around to find my tormentor and realized I had been struck by a golf ball. Henry had shanked his shot and found me instead.

Mr. Chen broke up. The fact that Henry had hit his boss struck his funny bone. I laughed too, and Henry apologized until I told him that was enough and I wasn't going to attempt to take equal revenge. The ice was finally broken, and, as the round continued, Mr. Chen began to describe a current project in Chengdu. The size of the project was typical for China but still staggering to me: 5,000 units of housing on a site that had been industrial space, with a historic river running through it. An American firm was currently working on it, but Mr. Chen indicated he wasn't all that happy with what they had shown him so far.

"Why don't you put something together and tell me how you would approach it?" he suggested.

Henry and I met later, and I got some more details. First of all, the work we would be doing would be without compensation — the Chinese

LEFT FROM LEFT, HENRY ZENG, THE AUTHOR, AND EDWIN GONZALES, AN ASSOCIATE, IN THE FORBIDDEN CITY ON THEIR FIRST VISIT TO CHINA.

RIGHT THIRD FROM LEFT, MR CHEN, 2ND FROM RIGHT, HENRY ZENG, AND THE AUTHOR AT THE TEE, WITH 3 OF THEIR 9 CADDIES.

developers often want a free taste. But this was the opportunity we wanted: a prestigious project with a major developer. We needed to go for it.

Besides not getting paid, the other big lesson for us would be getting used to the highly compressed timelines that were normal in China. Mr. Chen expected to see something in two weeks.

I flew in key talent from our offices in California. Our tiny garage-sized office, with no air conditioning and almost no design equipment, became our brutal around-the-clock sweatshop. But at least we knew what we were doing. I knew little about design norms in China, but I thought what we had done so successfully in California would translate well to China.

Late one evening we received the call: we were summoned to meet with Mr. Chen and the rest of the OCT team at 10PM that night. By then, their team would have been meeting, eating, and drinking all evening. It was not the ideal presentation time or format, but with all the decision makers in one place at the same time — an unusual occurrence — this was our shot, so we grabbed it.

We pulled a free table over to where Mr. Chen and his group were finishing an opulent feast. At first, when we began to present, they were

still chatting among themselves, but when Mr. Chen raised a single finger they fell silent. I spoke much of the time, and Henry translated. I explained that we had envisioned a community that integrated the buildings into what would become a beautiful landscape. I suggested that we change the course of the river here and there to bring it into harmony with the community: to enhance the clubhouse (often the central building in these types of projects), and to create a perfectly staged arrival experience for the first-time visitor. We showed how an entrance over a bridge would set the tone for how people would feel about this special place. Our materials would complement the landscape — rich, warm, and natural. Ever concerned with the community we would be shaping, I described places where people would gather together in harmony with the site's historic river.

We knew we were taking a risk. Our design approach was intentionally shocking, in stark contrast with the typical flashy, look-at-me, concrete and glass designs so prevalent in Asia. Our design was harmonious, historically informed and sensitive, warm, and low key. If we were to become successful in China we would want to be designing work that reflected our values.

When we finished, I simply stopped talking. Henry knew not to try

LEFT CROWDED INTO OUR FIRST OFFICE, OUR TEAM, DRAWN FROM THE U.S. AND LOCAL ARCHITECTS.

RIGHT FROM LEFT, THE AUTHOR, MR. CHEN, AND HENRY AT THE OPENING OF OUR OFFICE ON FERGUSON LANE, FRENCH CONCESSION, SHANGHAI.

SKETCHES FOR THE PROJECT IN CHENGDU FOR MR. CHEN, WHICH EVENTUALLY BECAME 5,000 HOMES.

TOP AND ABOVE OUR EXPRESSION OF A CALIFORNIA-STYLE INTEGRATION OF BUILDING AND LANDSCAPE, CLOSE TO THE RIVER THAT WOUND THROUGH THE SITE.

LEFT THE TOWER WE SUGGESTED, WHICH BECAME THE ESSENTIAL VISIT FOR ALL PROSPECTIVE BUYERS.

and fill in the gaps with nervous small talk, so he also stood there quietly, ready for anything.

And then Mr. Chen turned to his group and spoke, in Chinese in that quiet way of his. I couldn't for the life of me get a sense of what he was telling them. Henry, for his part, was expressionless, adding to my torture. Then Mr. Chen turned to us, and spoke in Chinese to Henry. Henry, listened without smiling, nodded, and finally turned to me to translate: "He said, 'Gentlemen, meet our new architects.'"

We had done it.

Our Grand Tour

Before long, Mr. Chen became our champion. We never knew exactly where he might be in China at any one moment, but he always seemed to know where we were. It was not an uncommon occurrence to receive a phone call in a random city on any given night telling Henry that Mr. Chen was in town, and wished us to join him for dinner.

Whenever we were summoned, Henry and I would dutifully report to the banquet location, where we would usually find Mr. Chen and his lieutenants, all smoking cigars and enjoying abundant delicacies as good French wine flowed freely. We were customarily asked to sit to Mr. Chen's right — a place of honor — and he would introduce us to all in attendance. Often, within a few days, we'd receive a call commissioning us to do another OCT project.

Each project provided us an opportunity to bring our values to the table. We were asked to propose some ideas for what was then known as Shanghai Block 13. The developers were a little lost, since there was an oversupply of typical housing, and yet they didn't only want to build office buildings. We poked around the community to try to understand what unmet needs there were. Before long, we discovered an untouched market: single men who wanted to

UNUSUALLY TRANQUIL FOR CHINA, THESE HOMES OFFER A SOFTER WAY TO LIVE IN CHENGDU.

OPPOSITE THE TOWER, THE CLUBHOUSE, AND PIERS FOR SMALL RECREATIONAL BOATS.

OPPOSITE AND BELOW SHANGHAI: MICRO UNIT STARTER HOMES FOR YOUNG COUPLES REPRESENTED A BREAKTHROUGH IN AFFORDABILITY.

BOTTOM TYPICAL MICRO UNIT INTERIOR, SLEEPING ABOVE, ONE SIMPLE BUT DYNAMIC ROOM.

get married, who could not yet afford a standard two- or three-bedroom condo, but whose prospective brides were turned off at the prospect of having to move in with their groom's parents.

What to do?

We proposed creating a new kind of dwelling for couples, something not before seen in China. We knew how to create very small apartments, now known as "micro units," that had style and dignity, and were basically one, not very large room. An overlook became the sleeping loft, internal glass kept the feeling open, and the general feeling was vastly more appealing than a room at one's folks. The design worked, the first project connected, and micro units for couples appeared in China. More recently, micro units have become a huge success in the United States.

No matter what the project, we were always looking to solve the challenge of how people would eventually form a community as they settled down in what we had designed. In most instances we would create a clubhouse — both to give a community a unique flagship design to be proud of, and an essential community hub where neighbors could meet and friendships take form.

We had sketched our Tianjin Clubhouse as something nautical, light, and airy to go with its water-surrounded location. At the time, the go-to building material was concrete, faced with local brick. Sufficient labor forces were always ready to carry the concrete on their shoulders, and everyone knew how to work with it. But we were concerned that concrete-only would give the clubhouse a heavy feeling, almost like an anchor that might sink into the water. We wanted light and airy. We wanted steel and glass.

Initially the pushback was total, but our team found a fabricator who could pre-assemble major sections off-site, and we showed our partners we could save both time and money with steel as opposed to concrete. They agreed, and, within a week, our team and the fabricators had designed the structure. From the moment it went up, it became a model of what an alternative to concrete might be.

Typically in China at the time, redevelopment meant mapping out the desired area and bulldozing it flat. The site of OCT Suzhou Creek in Shanghai — seemed destined for the same fate. But we were intrigued with the waterfront community's history. This was where the Japanese had begun their World War II assault on China. We felt the location was sacred, and that a new community needed to be anchored in a sense of that history.

At first our efforts to take our cue from what was already there were met with skepticism. But as we unfolded our plans, our Chinese clients could see that by respecting history we had almost automatically deepened the design. We were not creating a new "no where," but instead a community that was attached to its place and resonated with history — while still being new.

OCT ultimately took us to Chengdu, Shanghai, Wuhan, Dalian, and Tianjin to design similar, massive-scale, mixed-use projects that incorporated housing, offices retail, schools, and entertainment. Mr. Chen had become our Chinese Godfather, directing some $3 billion in projects to us, and helping us build our reputation.

LEFT OCT TIANJIN, WITH THE CLUBHOUSE, LOWER LEFT. THE HIGH RISES, UPPER LEFT, WERE COMPLETED IN THE SECOND PHASE OF THE PROJECT.

TRADITION REQUIRED THAT WE WORK IN THE LOCAL BRICK, AND THAT WE EVOKE THE REGIONAL STYLE, WHICH IS SOMEWHAT GOTHIC. THE PROJECT INCLUDES SCHOOLS, PUBLIC BUILDINGS, SHOPPING, 5,000 RESIDENCES, AND A CLUBHOUSE ON THE LAKE. THE POOL WAS BUILT WITH A LACY USE OF STEEL, A DEPARTURE FROM THE CUSTOMARY CONCRETE.

42街坊
BLOCK 42
41街坊
BLOCK 41
3街坊
BLOCK 3
苏州河
SUZHOU CREEK
苏州河
SUZHOU CREEK

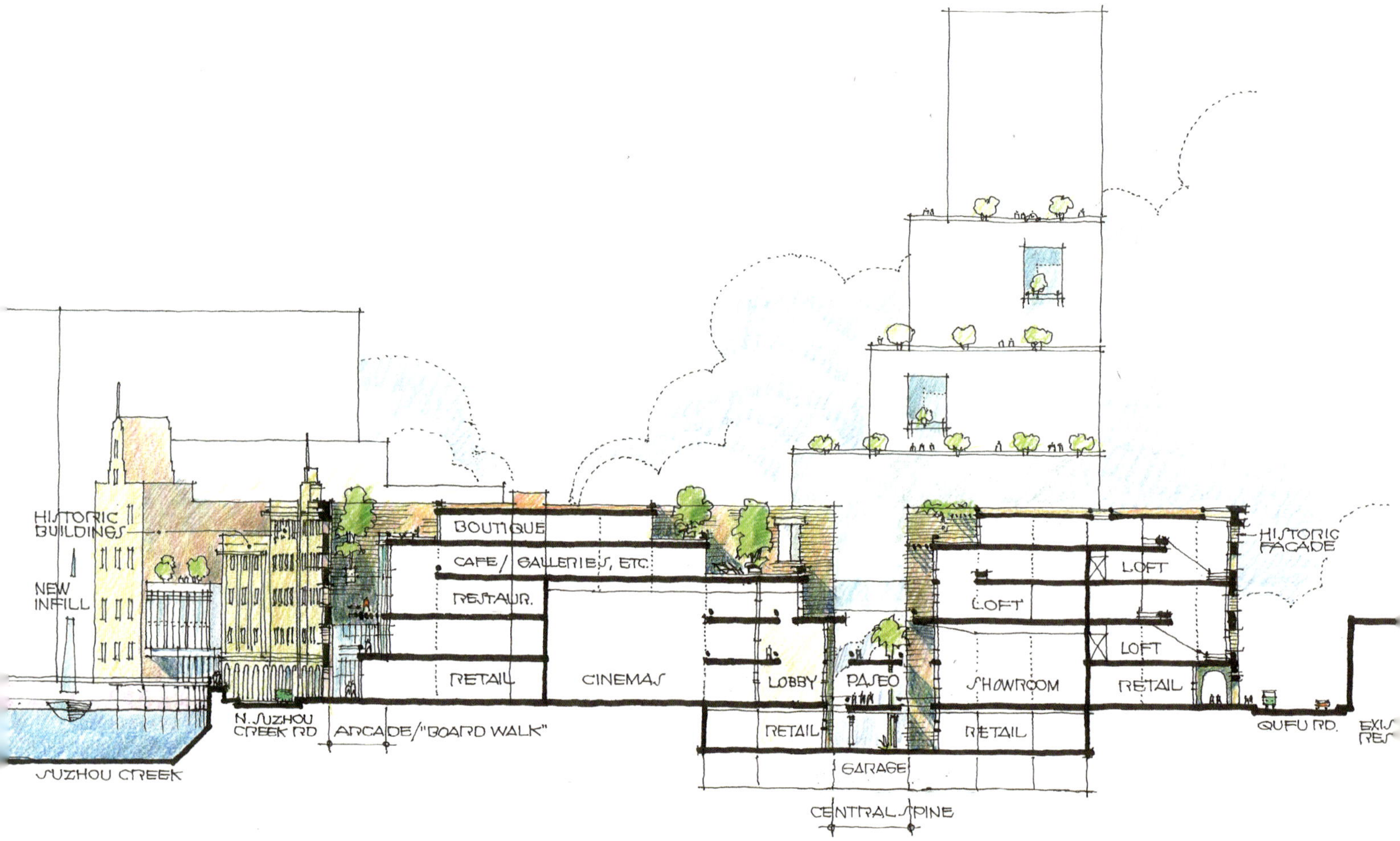
HISTORIC BUILDINGS
NEW INFILL
BOUTIQUE
CAFE/ GALLERIES, ETC.
RESTAUR.
RETAIL
CINEMAS
LOBBY
PASEO
SHOWROOM
RETAIL
LOFT
LOFT
LOFT
HISTORIC FACADE
N. SUZHOU CREEK RD
ARCADE/"BOARD WALK"
RETAIL
RETAIL
GARAGE
CENTRAL SPINE
QUFU RD.
SUZHOU CREEK

SUZHOU CREEK, SHANGHAI. THIS WAS THE HISTORIC SITE OF A JAPANESE ATTACK, WHICH BECAME KNOWN AS THE BATTLE OF SHANGHAI, WHERE JAPAN BEGAN ITS WAR ON CHINA. WE WON THE COMPETITION WITH OUR PLAN TO PRESERVE SIGNIFICANT PORTIONS OF THE HISTORIC WATERFRONT, AN UNUSUAL APPROACH AT THE TIME.

The Great Handshake

Our growing status led to our being invited to make a proposal for the provisional government of Changsha, which had partnered with a private developer called the Songya Lake Company in a massive public works effort to rechannel the famous Liuyang River and its adjacent wetlands. Together they were planning to develop a huge new city of 80 million square feet of building space — equal to a third of all the office space in midtown Manhattan — on 7,000 acres.

Changsha, on the Xiang River, is associated with the youth of Mao Zedong, the founding father of the People's Republic of China, and was now home to seven million residents.

The total built space would include an ecological business district and high lake waterfront; a low-rise residential community mixed with generous green public spaces; and an entertainment district with high-density, mid- and high-rise towers.

Each invited firm had six weeks to prepare concept drawings, models, and videos.

The scope of the project was so enormous that it was almost impossible to wrap our minds around it. The jump in scale raised an important issue: how would the person-made interventions interface with the lake? We structured a circulation system full of variation and interest, shaping a wide variety of distinctive areas and neighborhoods. And we preserved as much open space as possible.

Being a foreign expert was a double-edged sword. Although I brought the prestige of being an American architect, I could hardly understand the nuances of the client's vision. In this instance, I thought it was best not to get too tightly constrained by vast quantities of data. I felt we should develop a vision of a vibrant and inclusive city, offering rich experiences, and stick with it.

THE AUTHOR PRESENTING TO THE SONGYA LAKE COMPANY AND THE PROVISIONAL GOVERNMENT OF CHANGSHA.

I relied on my beliefs that underneath it all, no matter how great the scale, our task was to constantly think of the communities, and create opportunities for our future residents to make strong social connection. We wanted our new city to co-exist with nature — both in tension and in harmony.

The night before the presentations, we arrived, along with representatives of the other competing firms, at an aging, resort hotel. We were escorted to an enormous ceremonial ballroom as tall as it was wide. Formal, symmetric, and military in style, holding the competition there seemed intended to make us feel insignificant. Seating was roped off for the various constituent stakeholders who would review our ideas the next day: the military, the national government, the provincial government, and the press.

I watched several of the other teams present their visions. They were all stunning and futuristic — shiny skyscrapers standing amidst a hard-edged grid of streets and highways. The glitter was mesmerizing, fantastic, and ultimately, with no sense of human presence, mind-numbing.

When I was called to present, I focused on a metaphor drawn from what I had discerned from human scale and from the landscape itself: an intertwining of the fingers of various waterways with the fingers of land between them. We would be creating a grand handshake. Together, our Western firm would work with the Chinese development group, uniting our two cultures, East and West, creating harmony between natural and

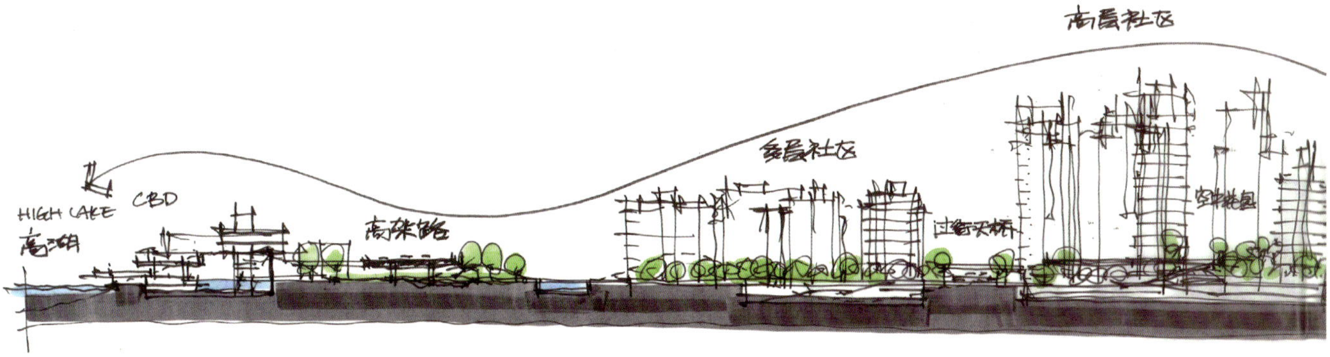

TOP THE HEIGHT OF THE BUILDINGS CREATES A FLOW DOWN TOWARD THE LAKE, TO THE LEFT.

ABOVE THE DESIGN'S TOTAL LAND AREA IS 3 SQUARE MILES.

structural elements, and learning from one another as we forged ahead.

We proposed utilizing the tributaries as fingers to define boundaries, to create opportunities for connection with the lake, and to link a variety of neighborhoods variously focused on people and how they would conduct commerce, enjoy entertainment, and feel about their dwellings.

I then moved on to what I hoped would be my "sticky landing."

"For the last 70 years our firm has been the go-to architects in Silicon Valley," I told the selection panel. "We're here to share with you the lessons learned in the innovation capital of the world. With our help you will become more competitive in a global marketplace."

The room did not erupt in cheers or applause. Our competitors did not hang their heads in defeat. The next team was called up, and we watched another wave of fantastic shiny visions.

The next morning as we prepared to leave for the airport, a friend of Henry's sent him a WeChat message: "You'd better start looking for office space here in Changsha," it said. We had won.

N
0
100m
200m
300m
400m
500

THE PROJECT WOULD EVENTUALLY BUILD 63 MILLION SQUARE FEET OF RESIDENTIAL SPACE, 5.5 MILLION SQUARE FEET OF OFFICE SPACE, AND 4 MILLION SQUARE FEET OF RETAIL, PLUS PUBLIC BUILDINGS.

Oxford Comes to the Yangzi River

We did not win every project we pitched. And we did not find success with every project we did win. Dozens of prospective clients found us, many seeking our help in building senior living communities. Thanks to national and international media showcasing Classic Residences by Hyatt, almost all the senior living developers I met in China showed me pictures of the Stanford project, holding it up as the gold standard by which they would measure their own projects. They noted the sensitivity and respect for the special needs of seniors. Through translators, and as much English as they could muster, they registered their understanding and appreciation of architecture that had successfully created thriving senior communities. Shamelessly, I would let them gush on and on before finally explaining, "I understand that project. I was the architect. My parents live there. Maybe you'd like a tour?"

With an aging population that will soon exceed the total U.S. population, China is confronting a significant social issue, and senior housing is a major component. The one-child policy in place from 1979 to 2015 created the phenomena known as 4-2-1, where four grandparents, together with their two adult children, were now raising a single child. Four-two-one was now turning around, and the single children were facing the prospect of supporting up to four grandparents, two parents, and as many children as they had of their own.

One of the early real-estate pioneers in senior housing was the Shanghai Industrial Investment Corporation (SIIC), which controlled thousands of acres of land on an island 90 miles north of Shanghai, where the mouth of the Yangzi River empties into the East China Sea. SIIC imagined its first senior living project as an intergenerational continuing-care retirement community intended to meet the burgeoning needs of the elderly that would serve as a model to the country. We were selected as project architect.

Not long into the design process I discovered that I actually had not one, but two clients — the one I knew and a second, never visible but ever-present client whose name was not on the contract: the People's Republic of China.

My SIIC colleagues were initially receptive to my Western ideas, but invariably — echoing the experience I had working with Stanford — they returned to the table suspicious of any senior-care concepts not yet introduced in China. This led to exhaustive studies of alternatives, adding years to the process.

Unfortunately, our visions for the actual feel of the community veered off in radically opposite directions. The client was intractable about mimicking the success from Stanford, wanting in this case to mimic the look of the University of Oxford. This was in absolute violation of my beliefs about context, recognizing the need to connect authentically with time and place, and in harmony with nature. But no matter how many times I tried to redirect the vision, the client remained deaf to my counsel.

This was not the first time that I had run up against what might well be one of the Negative Realities of Architecture, which in this instance was "He who writes the check has the power to call the shots." Over the years I had developed considerable skills in triumphing over this unpleasant reality, but the client held fast to his Oxford fixation. For me it was the antithesis of striving for perfection, but I finally accepted defeat.

I contemplated quitting, but by this time I was too invested in the project to abandon it.

However for our firm, the Shanghai project was a staggering success, quickly becoming the prototype for large-scale senior communities in China. The mammoth government-backed insurance companies — China Life, for whom we did the Yang Cheng Lake Island project, China Pacific, and Taikang — absorbing our values based on human-scale developments that met the individual's needs for community, ultimately transformed the way tens of thousands of Chinese seniors would live. The ideas we had originated in California had taken root in China.

From the perspective of my deep belief that architecture needs to respect place, to understand the conversation that it is either continuing or interrupting, Oxford on the Yangzi River was a great failure. I have never visited the completed community. Only recently could I bring myself to even look at a photograph of it.

FIRST PHASE OF THE YANG CHENG LAKE ISLAND SENIOR LIVING PROJECT, WHICH WILL EVENTUALLY OCCUPY THE ENTIRE ISLAND.

RIGHT THE PRESERVATION OF OPEN SPACES BECAME A SIGNIFICANT ASPECT OF THE DESIGN, DEDICATED TO THE SPIRITUAL, EMOTIONAL, AND PHYSICAL WELL-BEING OF ITS RESIDENTS.

BELOW THE ANGLED ROOFS ARE POSITIONED TO BOTH CAPTURE SOLAR ENERGY AND PROVIDE FILTERED LIGHT TO THE OPEN AREAS BELOW.

OPPOSITE THE FOLDING ROOF AND FAÇADE ACKNOWLEDGES THE TRADITIONAL REGIONAL HUI STYLE.

We Find Our Wall

Among the largest development companies in China was Wanda Group, a multinational conglomerate established in 1988 and focused on real-estate development, later branching out to become one of the world's leading sports and entertainment companies as well. Wanda had been founded by Mr. Wang Jianlin, whom *The Economist* called "a man of Napoleonic ambition," citing his background in the People's Liberation Army, where he had risen from border guard to regimental commander. Mr. Jianlin enforced iron discipline in his workplace.

As people in China began to amass more disposable income, Wanda partnered with the government to create large resort communities throughout the country to capitalize on the growing domestic travel industry. Generally situated around a lake, these resorts, dubbed "Dream Cities," included multiple hotels of various price points, entertainment centers, clubs, and restaurants.

By luck, our business development manager in China had been dating someone in a local leadership position at Wanda. She made an introduction, which led to an invitation to compete for the commission to master plan what eventually evolved into the first of 30 hotels in Dream City developments throughout China.

Working for one of the most successful, most admired brands in China was quite a coup. Because so much of the work was generated by our staff in Beijing, I was not involved in all of the details of the Wanda projects, but periodically I traveled to Beijing to check in, offer input, and put my stamp of approval on the work our group was doing.

On one such trip, we took the leaders of the Wanda team out for an upscale lunch to demonstrate our appreciation. As a late start compounded by slow restaurant service pushed the clock toward the one-hour mark, most of our Wanda guests got up and left the table before

OPPOSITE THE WANDA VISTA NEW CHANG HOTEL.

BELOW THE PORTE-COCHÈRE LEADS TO AN EVEN MORE IMPRESSIVE LOBBY.

the food arrived, to return to work. They would be docked half a day's pay if they were late, and the elegant lunch was not worth risking their income, let alone their jobs. It started to dawn on me that Wanda's work culture was largely based on fear.

When we were first hired, Wanda executives initially insisted on camping out in our small office to oversee our work. Later, they demanded our team work in their Beijing office under all the oppressive terms that governed their own staff. Grown men actually cried as Wanda supervisors refused to let them go home from the office at night. They worked from 9AM to 3AM and were expected back at their drafting tables again at 9AM the same morning. A bully mentality prevailed.

Wanda was powerful, developing some of the biggest, most interesting projects in the country. But they abused our people.

Although Wanda now understood that they could rely on us, before long we had reached our limit with a partner we no longer admired nor respected. We completed our last Wanda project, the Wanda Vista New Chang Hotel, a palatial six-star hotel with personal valets for each of its rooms, and accepted no more.

The Bamboo Clubhouse

It took me a while to realize that securing new work was not only based on the strength of our proposal but also on the strength of our relationships. Henry's relationship with Mr. Chen launched our efforts in China. Over time, I was able to build my own circles of trust with several of our Chinese business associates.

Among those with whom I found genuine friendship was Mr. Du, a successful developer from Chengdu.

When Mr. Du bought a large parcel of land in the newly developing Zhengxing district, he hired us to design a master plan for it. The mammoth project included six high-rise residential towers, a multistory shopping mall, and low-rise housing along the river. At my constant urging, along with the development of the master plan, Mr. Du finally agreed that a shared community building could bond the varied uses spread out over the rolling terrain into a stronger, more interconnected community.

But unfortunately, by the time Mr. Du agreed, we had allocated almost all of the site's square footage to revenue-producing uses, leaving no land for the clubhouse building I had lobbied so hard to include.

LEFT ZHENGXING: THREE RESIDENTIAL TOWERS OVER A SHOPPING MALL.

RIGHT THE OTHER THREE TOWERS, ACROSS THE RIVER.

Not very practical as a building site was a steep, landscaped hillside that acted as a view corridor rolling down toward the river.

A structure on that open space would impinge on the luxury towers' view of the water. When I was trying to find a way to save my clubhouse, I needed to find a way to both hide it and yet make it authentic to the area. Chengdu is famous for being the home of the panda, and pandas thrive in Chengdu because of its bamboo forests. So I proposed an alternative for the clubhouse: sinking the building below ground, like a cave in a bamboo forest, notched into the hill, with the landscape remaining intact as the roof.

Mr. Du embraced this idea and the two of us set about designing a little underground jewel box that sparkled with my laws of context, choreography, nature, storytelling, and art.

From then on, our monthly design review meetings attended by dozens of participants, including people from our San Francisco, Los Angeles, and Shanghai offices and spanning two full days, always began with a review of the progress on the clubhouse.

Blurring the boundaries between architecture, landscape, and interiors, the clubhouse creates moments of surprise and discovery through a creative reinterpretation of local Chengdu culture. Covered

with a grassy blanket of green terrain, the clubhouse is hardly visible to those approaching by foot or by car. The arrival experience emulates a walk through a bamboo forest, offering filtered light from above, and a grand atrium reminiscent of a forest clearing, with views of the creek outside.

Working in collaborative partnership over a long period of time, I became close with Mr. Du and his wife. One year, Alice and I invited them to our Palo Alto home for Thanksgiving. They helped stuff the turkey and prepare the side dishes for a party of 20 guests — a rare occasion for them, since the Chinese rarely entertain at home. It was a unique experience, indeed, for the Dus to celebrate an American, home-based, Thanksgiving holiday.

Later, when Alice joined me on a trip to Chengdu, Mr. Du arranged an extraordinary schedule of tours, banquets, Chinese opera, and a private tour of the Chengdu Research Base of Giant Panda Breeding — including the opportunity to hold the baby pandas.

A framed photo of Alice holding a baby panda in her arms is prominently displayed in our home library, a treasured keepsake of the intimate friendship I share with Mr. and Mrs. Du.

BELOW LEFT THE PLAN FOR ZHENGXING, WITH THE CLUBHOUSE HIDDEN ALONG THE RIVER.

BELOW RIGHT THE LANDSCAPE PARTI FOR THE CLUBHOUSE, WHICH WILL FIT UNDERNEATH THE GREEN ROOF.

BOTTOM THE MODEL OF THE CLUBHOUSE, GIVING SHAPE TO THE LANDSCAPE PLAN.

OVERLEAF THE CLUBHOUSE FROM THE CREEK.

Working in China, it often looked to me like effort in and for itself was often valued more than output: looking busy in itself was highly valued. In one unforgettable instance, I watched in amazement as workers rushed to lay down fairly expensive carpet even though the windows had not yet arrived. I observed that if it rained, the carpet would be ruined. "Not a problem," I was told. More carpet would replace the ruined carpet, but at least everyone was busy.

I've always valued results over effort. Ultimately, the effort, time, and sacrifice required for us to expand into China was enormous. But the results were beyond my wildest dreams.

I had been able to test whether my laws might work across different cultures to help build dynamic communities, and do their part to heal the world. I had come to believe they passed that test.

I had experienced personal growth as well. Not only did I discover that the laws scaled from their early days and medium-size projects to some of the vast projects we were then guiding, but I had also learned that *I* had scaled over the decades, growing along with my practice. Although from time to time I had come perilously close, my reach had not yet exceeded my grasp.

LEFT THE ROOF AND SKYLIGHTS. BEHIND, THE TOWER BRINGS LIGHT TO THE LOBBY.

BELOW THE TERRACE AND INFINITY POOL, FACING THE RIVER.

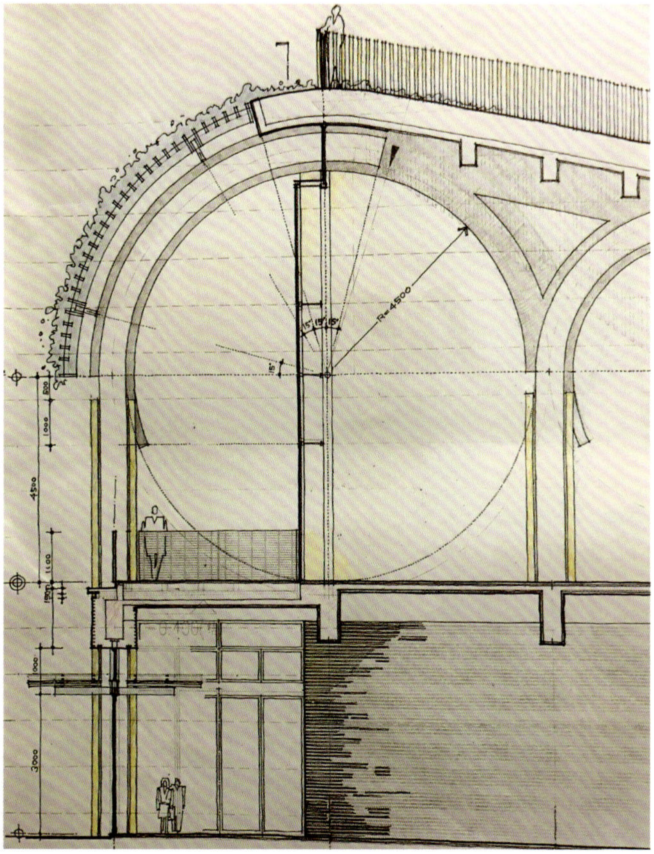

LEFT THE DRAWING SHOWS THE ARCH, BISECTED BY THE 9-METER-HIGH GLASS WALL.

BELOW LEFT THE FACE OF THE CAVE.

BELOW RIGHT THE ARCH BLURS THE SEPARATION BETWEEN INSIDE AND OUTSIDE.

ENTRANCE TO THE BAMBOO CAVE. TEXTURED STONE WALLS, BAMBOO ABOVE, AND OCCASIONAL PUDDLES.

THE ENTRANCE IS DELIBERATELY HIDDEN, CREATING A SUSPENSE FOR THE JOURNEY.

OPPOSITE THE RECEPTION DESK ACTS LIKE A BREAK IN THE FOREST.

BELOW THE STAIRS TO THE RECEPTION DESK LEAD UP TO A CLEARING BATHED IN A CANOPY-LIKE FILTERED LIGHT.

OVERLEAF THE UNDERGROUND LAGOON ALSO SERVES AS THE INDOOR POOL.

RIGHT DETAIL OF THE MIRO, NOW THE TALLEST BUILDINGS IN SAN JOSE, SHOWING THE TRANSITION FROM THE SMOOTH TO THE ROUGH FACE. TO THE LEFT OF THE MIRO, THE BUILDING WITH THE DARK-BLUE STAIR TOWER IS BY THE AUTHOR'S FATHER, C.1960S.

BELOW SITE PLAN. THE TWO PENTAGONAL TOWERS, WITH THEIR SMOOTH SURFACES WHEN IN CLOSE PROXIMITY TO EACH OTHER, RADIATING ENERGY TO THE DOWNTOWN, INCLUDING CITY HALL AT BOTTOM.

OPPOSITE WHERE THE TOWERS ARE IN CLOSE PROXIMITY, THEY SPEAK TO EACH OTHER AS FAMILY, WITH THEIR SMOOTH SURFACES. THEIR FACE TO THE WORLD IS BOLDER, CONTRIBUTING THEIR CONFIDENT VOICE TO A BUSTLING URBAN MOSAIC.

A global developer from Beijing had come to California to develop high rises in Silicon Valley, and my reputation in China brought us together in California. I designed two, 26-story, high-rise residential towers for them, the Miro. I can park in the Market Street garage of my youth, and walk to the Miro, a short distance of half a mile. And in the process of creating these towers, I have also been making a transition, as my father had before me. The firm that was once known for its Silicon Valley residences had become a global firm recognized for its work in planning, public interest, education, and residential, and was now about to become known as an innovative designer of high rises.

Since my passion for storytelling often found its expression in architecture, one might wonder what the Miro towers tell. If you look at their sparkling new surfaces, you might notice that the towers are distinctly smooth when they are close to each other. You might consider where else can we hope to enjoy such frictionless conversation? How about with members of our family. I think of the towers not as brothers (there might be too much sibling rivalry) but as cousins, sharing a lot of heritage in common, but each bringing something different to the world. And if we let our gaze continue to wander across the surfaces of the towers, we can't help but note that as they become more outward facing, they become a little more exuberant, even a bit brash. What is their tell? Maybe their public face is proud to be a new and optimistic voice in the complex chorus of voices rising up in Silicon Valley, ready to play its part, to provide homes for hundreds of people and give them a joyous place to live.

Why wonder, "If only these walls could speak?" In fact, if you look closely, they do.

BLACK
LIVES
VOICES
DREAMS
FUTURES
MATTER

THE AUTHOR AT QING CHENG MOUNTAIN.

My career in architecture began in San Jose, working on the Market Street Parking Garage, discovering the first of my 9 Realities: that architecture is the pursuit of perfection. As I worked on that project with my father, he was taking the first steps in transitioning the leadership of the practice to me. Over many years, he watched as I changed our focus from the residences that had been his passion, to my focus, driven to improve people's lives by shaping their communities. My work had taken me from California to China, and now our firm had offices in New York, Texas, California, and Shanghai.

Ten years before shifting from CEO to Chairman of my firm, I had agreed with David Hart that he would become the next CEO. He shared my passion for the potential of architecture to shape communities, and in our weekly Friday meetings we would often question which of our continually refined principles, now the 9 Realities, would be most useful in guiding us toward the optimal solution for any given challenge. By the time we were collaborating on the Miro, it was clear to me the time was right for what became a seamless transition.

On a strangely quiet Sunday in China, seeking respite from the chaos of the frenetic work pace we'd been maintaining in anticipation of yet another competition for a mega project commission, Henry and I treated ourselves to an uncharacteristic vacation day and ventured out of the city to Qing Cheng Mountain, the birthplace of Taoism, a spiritual retreat 30 minutes from Chengdu. The birds chirped, a heavy mist hovered, and saffron-robed monks carrying supply packs on their backs traversed the lake by ancient gondola. The atmosphere was mystical as the sun broke through the clouds — a rare occurrence in this fog-enshrouded mountain retreat so close in distance but so far in ambiance from the non-stop intensity of developing China.

I was so deep in thought that I nearly lost my footing when the long, slow, blast of a steam locomotive on my phone pierced the serenity of the moment. I heard my father's halting, tired voice on the line.

"Rob?" he asked. "Is that you? Where are you? What are you doing?"

At 86 years of age, my fight-to-the-death father, who had always had the answers, who had always ruled the roost, whose charm and innovation had won over Silicon Valley's cognoscenti, was calling from a hospital bed. Having wrestled with lung cancer in recent years, and suffered a fall a few months back, he was calling to tell me he had reached a decision.

"No more interventions," he said. "I've lived a good life. The time has come."

This was so unlike my father.

He sounded weary. But he sounded content.

From my perch on the mountainside, I almost felt like I was in Heaven and Goody was calling to say he would soon be on his way. The contrast between the transcendent setting, the shrill train sound, and my father's words of resignation were difficult to process.

I quickly tried to calculate how long would it take me to climb down the mountain. How much time would I need to pack up? How soon could I catch a flight? A presentation, which had brought me to China, was scheduled for the day after tomorrow. I was unsure what to do about that. I hardly realized I was muttering all of this aloud, when the sound of my father's voice cut me off.

"No, no, no, no," Goody said. "I'm fine. You stay there and do your presentation. I'll see you later this week, when you're home, as scheduled."

I was a little uneasy proceeding with business as usual when my father was lying in a hospital and had made what seemed to me to be a monumental, life-and-death decision. But he reassured me, as was his way.

LEFT THE BOAT ON YUECHENG LAKE, CROSSING TO THE MOUNTAIN.

RIGHT THE ASCENT.

"We have both been blessed to have shared a lot of time together," he said. "There are no words and no subjects that we haven't discussed and resolved. There is no unfinished business. There is nothing more we need to say."

I couldn't help but marvel to myself at how much my relationship with my father contrasted with my relationship with my own son, whose life was so suddenly cut short that we were left with a lifetime of words and experiences left unsaid and undone.

"All right," I reluctantly agreed. It had never been much use arguing with Goody. "I'll see you at the end of the week."

A few hours later, when I got down the mountain, the locomotive on my phone blew once again.

It was my wife, Alice, calling with news from home.

In the few hours since I had spoken to him, my father, my mentor, my partner Goody had peacefully, quietly passed away.

LAGNIAPPE

A Utopia for the Automobile

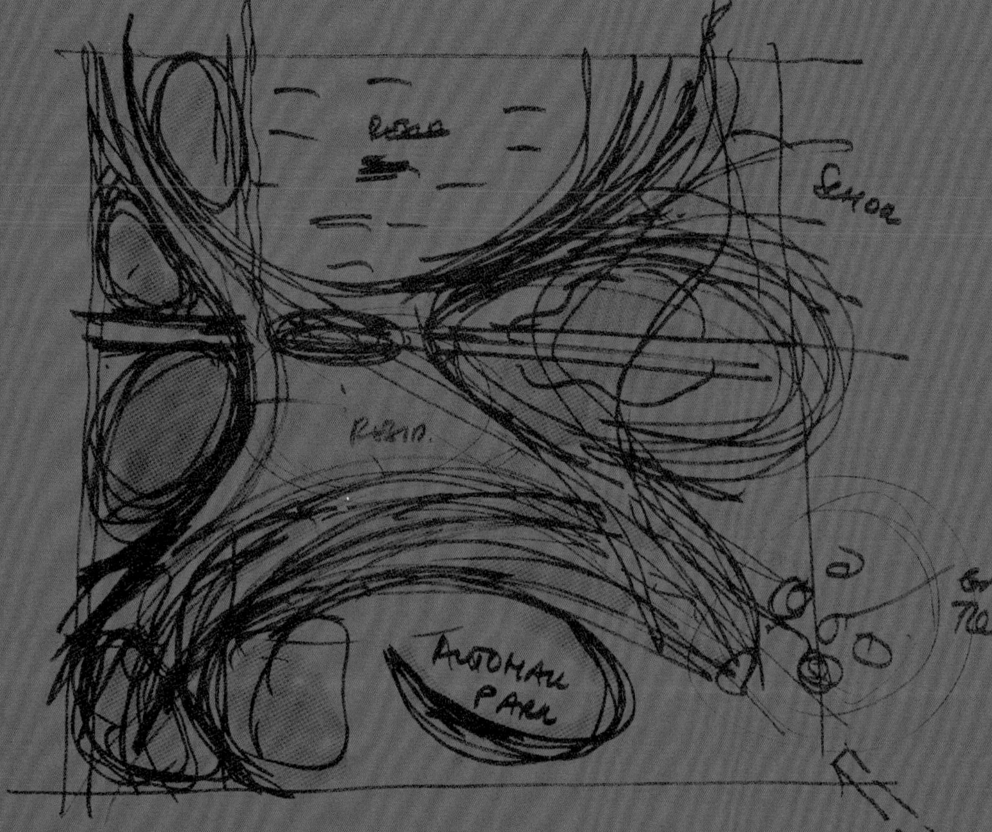

When new eras begin, architecture tends toward the utopian. China, in the early decades of the twenty-first century, began to internalize its recent and astounding financial growth. The architecture of the era became unleashed, fettered only by the limits of materials and imaginations.

Tianjin is the fourth largest city in the country and the largest coastal city in northern China. For the Tiefangnanlu Development Competition, we unleashed ourselves. The district, when we began, was the old automobile center of the city, where one could buy a new or used car, get any kind of part, and have repairs from the highest quality down to guys bashing out dents on street corners.

For our proposal, we were inspired by the first waves of romantic automotive design — the 1920s with their lavish use of brass and leather, and then the postwar era, which brought forth land-yachts of fantastic displays of chrome and color. And we were inspired by winding roads, the most beautiful kinds of journeys that only the automobile made possible.

We were also driven to undo the vast damage across the planet that the automobile revolution had wrought: air pollution, congestion, and the demise of coherent urban life. We wanted to create a new space where the automobile could be becoming transformed into something compatible with the celebration of human needs for community, beauty, recreation, and green space.

Although we stunned the judging committee with our audacious proposal, our vision has not yet been transformed into reality. It remains just a vision, the only unbuilt work in this book.

In the French Quarter in New Orleans, after a good dinner, guests are often sent into the night with a little treat, a lagniappe, as they head out the door. This chapter is my lagniappe for you, Dear Reader.

FROM TOP
THE EXISTING AUTOMOBILE DISTRICT.

A 1957 CADILLAC EL DORADO BIARRITZ.

AN INSPIRATIONAL SWITCH-BACK WITH PERPETUAL HEADLIGHTS.

THE INTRICATE TAPESTRY OF A HIGH-FLYING INTERCHANGE.

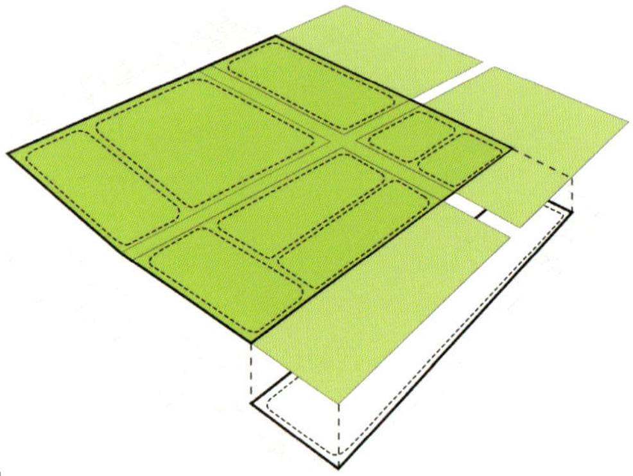

1

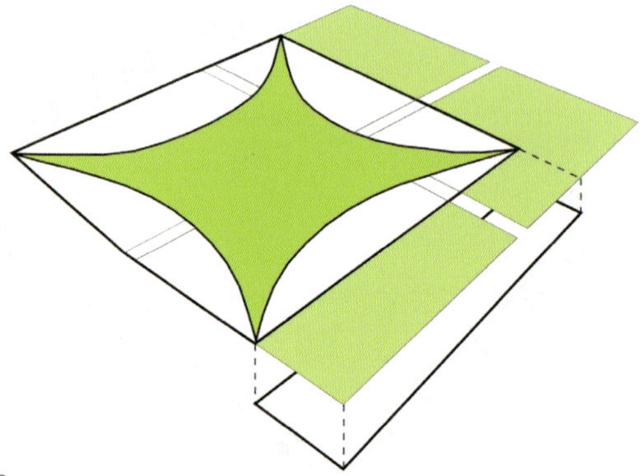

2

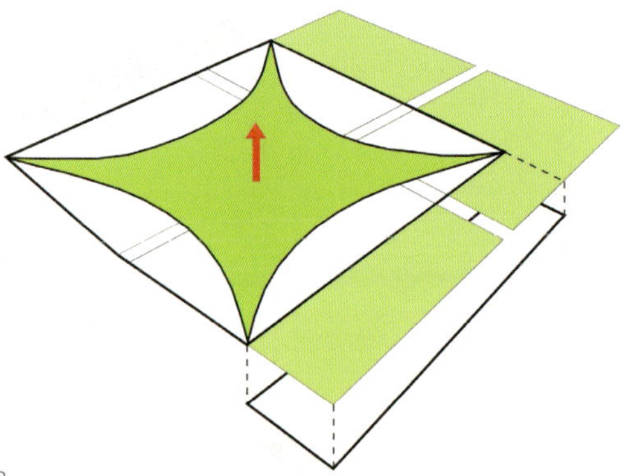

3

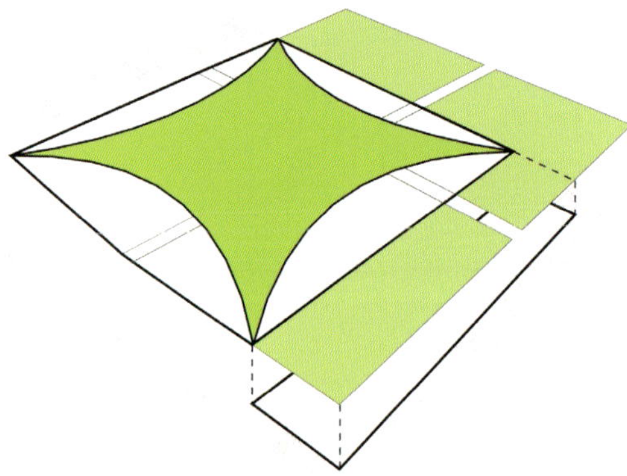

4

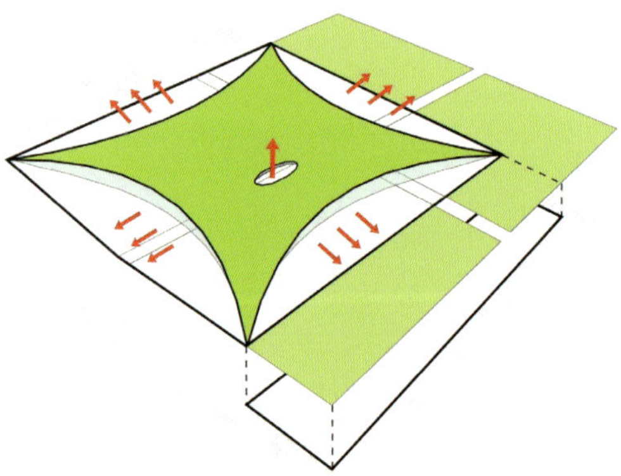

5

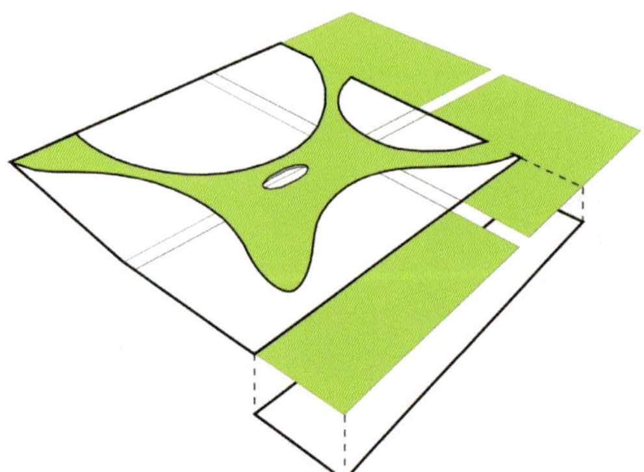

6

1 THE DARK GREEN AREA IS THE SITE, 8 MEGA BLOCKS DIVIDED BY TWO 10-LANE ROADS, WHICH WE COVERED WITH A "TARP."

2 BEGINNING TO SHAPE THE TARP, GROUNDED TO THE FOUR CORNERS OF THE SITE.

3 WE LIFTED THE TARP IN THE CENTER.

4 THE TARP BECOMES A MULTI-FUNCTIONAL SUSTAINABLE GREEN CANOPY.

5 WE PIERCED A HOLE (THE "OCULUS") TO BRING LIGHT TO THE SPACES BELOW. LIGHT ALSO ENTERS FROM THE SIDES.

6 WE REFINED THE TARP TO BECOME AN INTERCONNECTED PARK.

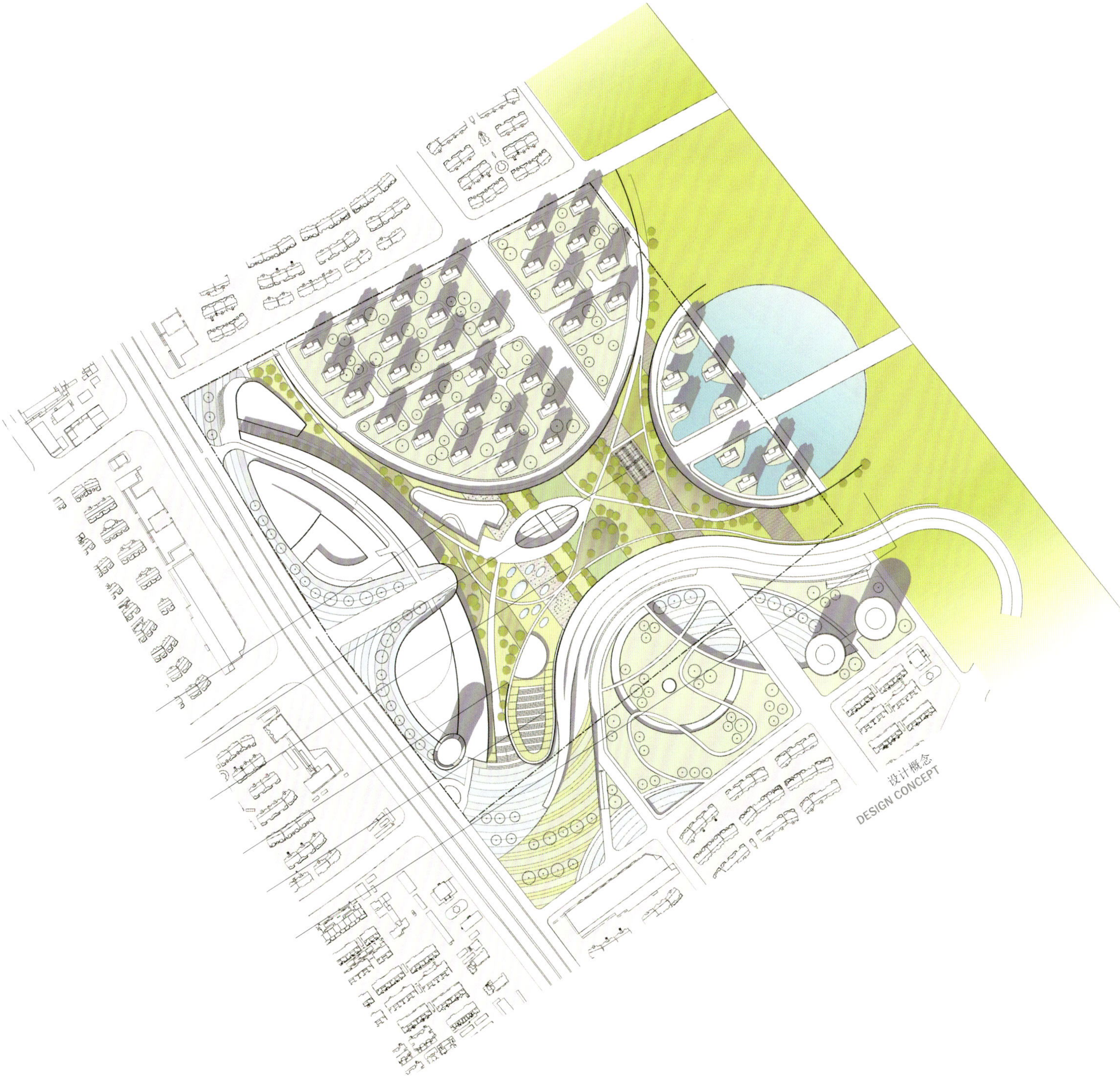

THE TWO MAJOR HIGHWAYS
NOW COULD PASS UNDER
THE PARK

THE PARK CANOPY, PIERCED BY THE OCULUS, WHICH BRINGS LIGHT TO THE GROUND LEVEL, WITH A RESIDENTIAL ENTRY DROP-OFF ON THE LEFT AND THE AUTOMOTIVE DISTRICT ON THE RIGHT. BELOW IS THE HIGH-SPEED FREEWAY, AND BELOW THAT IS RAIL.

DETAIL OF THE HUB UNDER THE OCULUS.

FROM TOP

THE ENTRY IS AT THE LOWER LEFT, PASSING THROUGH THE ARCED BUILDING, WHICH HOUSES RETAIL STORES, ENTERTAINMENT, OFFICES, AND A HOTEL.

CARS ON THE TEST-DRIVE RACETRACK. THE TOWER ON THE RIGHT STORES NEW CARS FOR DELIVERY AND THE TOWERS ON THE LEFT ARE RESIDENTIAL.

A WINTER SCENE. AUTOMOBILE SHOWROOMS ARE TUCKED INTO THE CANOPY. THE TEST-TRACK WINDS AROUND THE PARK.

FROM TOP

THE THEATER, ON THE LEFT. ON THE RIGHT, THE OFFICE TOWER AND HOTEL. IN BETWEEN, THE STAIRCASE LEADS UP TO THE PARK CANOPY.

THE PORTE-COCHÈRE IS FOR THE HIGH-RISE OFFICE HOTEL. JUST TO THE RIGHT ARE THE AUTOMOBILE SHOWROOMS.

FROM A RESIDENTIAL TERRACE, A VIEW TOWARD THE LUXURY RESIDENTIAL STANDING IN THEIR LAKE.

THE RESIDENTIAL COMMONS UNDERNEATH THE PARK CANOPY.

THE OFFICE TOWER, SHOWING THE SHAPE DETERMINED BY THE CURVING ALGAE TUBES THAT CONVERT CARBON DIOXIDE TO OXYGEN. TO THE UPPER LEFT, THE AMPHITHEATER IS ABOVE THE AUTOMOTIVE SHOWROOM; THE OCULUS IS IN THE CENTER, AND THE RESIDENTIAL COMMONS, ON THE RIGHT, CARVED INTO THE CANOPY.

ACKNOWLEDGMENTS

I HAVE BEEN MOST FORTUNATE TO HAVE ENJOYED A career working with hundreds of very talented colleagues, including my partner, Ernie Yamane, and trusted advisor and extraordinary problem solver, David Ewell, who have both worked alongside me for over 40 years. A special thank you to David Hart, President of Steinberg Hart, and Mike Miller, Design Director, both of whom have been instrumental in assisting me to develop and refine the 9 Realities. Without the accounting support of partner Frederick Braggs this project may have stalled along the journey.

Working with super creative designers reminds me of my experiences of riding my sister's Arabian stallion, Rebel. The interactions were intense, scary, and memorable. It has been my privilege to work with these extraordinary designers, each quite different but all of whom shared my passion for striving for perfection. Their contributions to the projects in the book were priceless. Thank you from the bottom of my heart Thuyen Nguyenphuc, my first ally in exploring the power of coupling graphic storytelling with text; Vladimir Frank for Job Corps, Davis Library, and the Private Residence; Dave Mitani for Fullerton; Richard Song for Markethouse Lofts; and Hong Chen and Henry Zeng for Classic Residences by Hyatt, the Campus for Jewish Life, and all the China projects.

Looking back, going to China turned out to be more challenging than I had anticipated. Traveling halfway around the world dozens of times, striving to understand a rich and storied culture that had evolved over centuries, I came to love China and consider it a second home. It was one of the most wild and crazy periods of my life. My trusted support system included David Nieh, Henry Zeng, Hong Chen, and Jason Briscoe, who through more challenges and adventures than imaginable, became and always will be my Chinese brothers.

Writing a book may seem like a solitary thing to do, but in my case I was very privileged to be supported by a talented group of professionals that shared my passion for storytelling, including my friend and collaborator Gerald Sindell, who turned the first draft of this book on its head; the extraordinary creative talent from Adam and Catherine Hooper of Hoop Design; the wisdom and perspective from Matt Cooke of Iron Creative; and the material development, patience, and encouragement from Susan Wolfe.

To collect and synthesize all the materials for the book required assistance from numerous colleagues with whom I was privileged to work in the U.S. and China. A special shout out to the above-and-beyond graphic support from the talented Corissa Hulick, as well as fact checking, graphic documentation, and research from Karen Jaimeson, Krystal Conklin, Deema Zahra, and Krisy Ye from our Shanghai office. Working seamlessly between Asia, the U.S., and the U.K. (Hoop Design) would never have been possible without the amazing IT support of Sargon Henderson.

Research, collateral retrieval, and memory support was graciously provided by Professors Ray Lifchez and Sam Davis from the College of Environmental Design at U.C. Berkeley; Elaine Schultz for the Market Street Garage; Teresa Alvarado, Leslie Gilroy, and Chandra Brooks for Job Corps; Todd Regonini for Markethouse Lofts; Barry Brukoff for the Private

Residence; Mike Smith for Fullerton; Laura Jones, Stanford University campus archaeologist for the Classic Residences by Hyatt; Shelly Hebert, Rick Rudman, Zack Broder, and Joey Felsen for the Taube Koret Campus for Jewish Life; and Leanne Li , Ted McMahon, and Edmond Rivera for MIRO.

I am particularly appreciative of the kind words and thoughtful foreword contributed by my dear friend, Penny Pritzker. I'd like to thank Amanda Fasenmyer for her gift of introducing me to Gerald Sindell; Doree Allen, founding director of Stanford's Oral Communication Program, for her invaluable input; and Russell Abraham, not only for his beautiful photography but also for his sustained support in helping to get the book published.

I would be terribly remiss to not humbly thank San Jose Mayor Sam Liccardo, Alicia John-Baptiste and SPUR, Mark Kroll, Lydia Tan, Lucy Li, Rick Swig, Rob & Di Master, George Chaltas, and Mike Smith for their precious time, contributions, coaching, and tireless moral support through this effort.

Lastly, I would like to thank my family for their love, support, and encouragement during the two years I spent fixated on completing my story. With special appreciation to my mother Gerry Steinberg, sister Joanie Laurence, brother Tom Steinberg, Sweet, Sweet Alice, Talia (Chocolate), and Rachel (Vanilla).

PHOTO CREDITS

EVERY EFFORT HAS BEEN MADE TO TRACE COPYRIGHT HOLDERS AND obtain permission to reproduce this material. Please do get in touch with any enquiries or any information relating to any image or rights holder. The author apologizes if any omissions have inadvertently been made.

Benny Chan pages 192, 193, 194, 195, 196, 197, 198, 199
Eric Figge pages 108, 111, 112, 113, 115, 116, 117
Gensler pages 38, 39
Hank Kranzler pages 12, 13
Hunter Kerhart pages 266, 267, 269, 270, 271, 272, 273
Jane Lidz pages 34, 35, 37
Jason Briscoe pages 264, 265
Jefferey Michael George pages 94, 95 (illustration)
John Linden pages 62, 63, 64, 65, 121, 139
Katrina Steube page 249 (top left and top right)
Mert Carpenter pages 71 (right), 72
Nicholas Reid pages 128, 129
Paul Dingman page 244 (top)
Prohl Studios pages 66, 67, 191, 212, 213
Rabbi Joey Felsen page 230
Richard Barnes pages 149, 152, 153, 154, 155, 156, 157, 158, 159, 160, 161, 162, 163, 164, 165, 166, 167, 168, 169, 170, 171, 172, 173
Rob Miller pages 74, 75, 76, 77, 78, 79, 80, 82, 83, 84, 85
Russell Abraham pages 6, 222 (top), 224, 225, 274, 275
Seth Powers pages 257, 258, 259
Steve Whittaker pages 66, 67, 109
Tim Hursley pages 96, 97, 98, 99, 100, 101, 102, 103
Tim Griffith pages 124, 125, 126, 127, 132, 133, 134, 135, 136, 137, 140, 141, 142, 143, 144, 145, 214, 215, 217, 218, 219, 220, 221, 222 (bottom), 223, 226, 227, 228, 229, 245, 246, 247, 249 (bottom right)
Zilinag Ni pages 248 (bottom), 249 (lower left)

INDEX

PAGE NUMBERS IN *ITALICS* REFER TO ILLUSTRATIONS

M

N

O

P

Q

S

ORO Editions
Publishers of Architecture, Art, and Design
Gordon Goff: Publisher

www.oroeditions.com
info@oroeditions.com

Published by ORO Editions

Copyright © 2021 Robert Tabin Steinberg

All rights reserved. No part of this book may be reproduced, stored in a retrieval system, or transmitted in any form or by any means, including electronic, mechanical, photocopying or microfilming, recording, or otherwise (except that copying permitted by Sections 107 and 108 of the U.S. Copyright Law and except by reviewers for the public press) without written permission from the publisher.

You must not circulate this book in any other binding or cover and you must impose this same condition on any acquirer.

Author: Robert Tabin Steinberg with Gerald Sindell
Book Design, Copy-editing and Pre-press: Hoop Design
www.hoopdesign.co.uk
Foreword: The Honorable Penny Pritzker
Managing Editor: Jake Anderson

10 9 8 7 6 5 4 3 2 1 First Edition

ISBN: 978-1-954081-31-4

Pre-Press by Pixel Colour Imaging Ltd., London
Color Separations and Printing: ORO Group Ltd.
Printed in China.

ORO Editions makes a continuous effort to minimize the overall carbon footprint of its publications. As part of this goal, ORO Editions, in association with Global ReLeaf, arranges to plant trees to replace those used in the manufacturing of the paper produced for its books. Global ReLeaf is an international campaign run by American Forests, one of the world's oldest nonprofit conservation organizations. Global ReLeaf is American Forests' education and action program that helps individuals, organizations, agencies, and corporations improve the local and global environment by planting and caring for trees.

www.howarchitecturetells.com
www.steinberghart.com
www.thoughtleadersintl.com